# THE OLD TESTAMENT
# WITHOUT ILLUSIONS

# THE OLD TESTAMENT
# WITHOUT ILLUSIONS

*by* JOHN L. McKENZIE

THE THOMAS MORE PRESS, *Chicago, Illinois*

Portions of this book appeared, in different form, in
the program "Keys: For a Richer Understanding of
the Bible," also published by the Thomas More Association.

Scripture quotations are from the Revised Standard
Version, Oxford University Press.

ISBN 0-88347-098-5

# Contents

# 1

## DID GOD WRITE THE BIBLE?

**W**ITH some reservations concerning how the reply should be formulated exactly, the whole of Christian tradition from the earliest centuries answers in a unanimous and uninterrupted affirmative. The First Vatican Council (1870) declared more clearly than any earlier council that the Sacred Scriptures, composed under the inspiration of the Holy Spirit, have God as their author. Hence the Bible is often designated as the word of God; hence it is called the sacred book.

The belief that God wrote the Bible existed in Judaism before Christian times and was accepted with no modification by the apostolic church. New Testament references to God's authorship of the Bible show a not surprising affinity in thought and in word to Jewish expressions of this belief. There are not many such references; this point of belief was not a matter of debate. Yet this belief is not founded in any claims which are made in any biblical book for itself.

Many passages in the Bible are credited to some form of divine influence, which may be called in some cases revelation and in other cases inspiration, preserving for each of these words the vagueness of definition which has made them so useful to theologians; but such a claim is not the same thing as the claim that God wrote the passages, still less the book. In fact the belief in the divine authorship of the Bible is a postbiblical belief, made necessary by a belief that the books of the Bible express the mind of God in a way in which no other book does. The belief put just in this way does not of necessity imply that God wrote the books. And in spite

7

of the origin of the Christian belief in the divine inspiration of
the Bible of Judaism, the Christian belief in its developed
form rejected most of the elements of the Jewish belief.

The long and solid belief in the divine authorship of the
Bible is combined in contemporary theology with a total lack
of a definition of inspiration, the name given to the unknown
process by which it is believed God wrote the books of the
Bible. It is no longer a matter of dispute among theologians
how inspiration is to be defined; it is rather a lack of interest in
the problem, a general feeling among theologians, sometimes explicit, that there is no solution to the problem, and
therefore it is not worth pursuing.

Now to maintain that God wrote the Bible and admit that
the process is not known is not a comfortable position for the
theologian, who conceives it to be his gift and his duty to
rationalize the articles of belief. It could even cause some to
wonder whether an article which is so totally beyond analysis
is really an article of faith. Perhaps it should be classified with
other articles of belief which the apostolic church uncritically
accepted, like the literary work of Moses and a flat earth
sandwiched between a heaven of bliss above and a hell of fire
beneath. We have, not without some anguish, adjusted faith
in the contemporary world with the realization that the examples given are unrealities. I do not think the contemporary
church is ready for this suggestion, and therefore I do not
make it. I merely wish to point out that such a position toward
biblical inspiration might be wrong, but it would not be un-
precedented.

The Jewish scribes of pre-Christian times and the Christians of apostolic and patristic times were not embarrassed by
a lack of definition of inspiration. The questions may be thus
phrased: If God is the author of the Bible, what did he do in

the composition of the Bible which he did not do in the composition of the Iliad? Plainly the books of the Bible have all the appearance of the work of human authors—like the Iliad. Whatever God did was done to the human author; and since the Bible itself gives no clue, the ancient scholars were left to their imagination; the question became not what God did but what could he do. He could feed words into the mind of the author, or even into his ear; whether it was done one way or the other, the human author became a stenographer. This meant that he ceased to be an author; the word of God was not the word of man. Or the author could be thrown into a trance, like the oracle of Delphi, whose words and voice were the words and voice of Apollo—or so it was believed; Apollo too was an unreality.

An early Christian author likened the biblical writer to the lyre on which the musician plays a tune; the theory is pretty, but what does it mean? This suggestion anticipated somewhat the theory of Thomistic theology in which the author was an instrumental cause (more accurately quasi-instrumental, almost but not quite an instrument), like the pen in the writer's hand. The theologians recognized that the biblical author was quite capable of writing a book without being a pen or a lyre or a stenographer; the pen does not write, the lyre does not sing, the stenographer does not record without their principal. The theologians responded that the man was capable of writing a book but not of writing the word of God, which on examination turns out to be an evasion. What did God do in writing the book of Genesis which he did not do in the Iliad? Unless we answer this, we are in danger of saying that the Bible is the word of God because it is so called.

It has become evident in recent times—and it is hard to see

why it took so long—that the theories of dictation or a trance or the lyre are not only indefensible but irrational. These theories deny the human author any part in the writing, and preserve God's authorship by removing human authorship. I do not mean to be irreverent when I say that a chimpanzee could be the author of a biblical book in this theory. But as long as the Bible was all equally the word of God, readers—even scholars—did not notice that when God dictated to Amos, the vocabulary, the sentences, the imagery and the cast of mind were different from what he dictated to Isaiah.

If one wants to push this idea to extremes, one may ask why the dictation of God to Amos and Isaiah was so far superior to his dictation to the author of the books of Chronicles. What did God do in the composition of Isaiah and Amos that he did not do in the composition of the books of Chronicles? What did he do in the composition of Psalm 23, universally esteemed as a jewel of world poetry, which he did not do in the composition of Psalm 119? Among these examples the books of Chronicles and Psalm 119, if they had been preserved without the belief in divine authorship, would be easily recognized for what they are, some of the worst writing ever done by anyone both in content and in style. It was difficult for Christians and Jews to admit that God as an author sometimes produced material which a modern pub-lisher would reject. Yet this obvious difference in the quality of biblical literature was serenely unnoticed; one does not criticize the writing of God Almighty.

The theory of the instrumental cause was an attempt to give due credit both to the divine and the human author. The question is, what is due credit. When the biblical books were venerated rather than read, or read in a translation which was often remarkably unfaithful to the original, it was not yet seen clearly that the books of the Bible show no sign that the activity of the human author was different from the activity of any other human author. If God was active, the book was to be totally attributed to two authors; and this could be done only if one of the authors was subordinate to the other. The official teaching of the Catholic church in recent times has been that the subordination was not a subordination of one who worked under another's command or received information from another or who submitted his work to the approval of another. If God was an "author," he had to do more than this. The question remains what did he do?

In recent times theologians have appealed to the analogy of the Incarnation to explain the divine authorship of the Bible through inspiration. Just as the two natures, divine and human, are united in the one person of the Word, so the human author is assumed by the divine author to produce a human book which is the word of God. The analogy is attractive but dangerous. In Christ, according to established theology, there are two natures and two operations, distinct and not confused. It is precisely the duality of operations, divine inspiration and human writing, which we are still unable to distinguish. The words and actions of the Incarnate Word were the words and actions of God, but they were entirely produced by human powers. It comes to this, perhaps to risk putting a fine point crudely; the Word was incarnate just by being and not by doing. This is not what has been meant by inspiration. It gives a different answer to our question, what did God do in the writing of the Bible which he did not do in the writing of other books; he did nothing, but he was present as he was not for other books.

Luis Alonzo-Schökel has drawn our attention to the social and historical character of language. When we learn a language, we join a community older than ourselves and sure to outlive us. Language is a given. It must be accepted as it is. A few great writers take liberties which lesser men may not take. The price of playing with language against the rules is loss of communication. One thinks of this when some enthusiastic social thinkers insist on the freedom of certain elements in our society to create their own language apart from the language of the establishment. When they do, they become unintelligible; or if they achieve intelligibility, it becomes apparent that they have nothing to say. Language is the means of learning as well as the means of communication; refusal to accept the language is refusal to learn. The linguistic society both enables us to express our minds as well as places limits on self-expression. Our ability to express our thoughts and feelings is limited by our control of the language.

Like the members of the language community, the community itself lives in history. The language changes without plan and without predictable direction. The modern reader and speaker of English cannot read fourteenth century English without some specialized study. If he were to engage in conversation with a contemporary of Chaucer, it would be like speaking a foreign language. The linguistic changes, we observed, are without plan or direction. They come because of changes in material and intellectual culture. Consider, for instance, how the automobile and the aircraft have altered our patterns of language and enlarged our vocabulary. Words become obsolete because the culture depends on quicker verbal communication or because the words designate obsolete objects. How many of our contemporaries can tell at once what is meant by a whiffletree? A frozen language is a dead language.

We noticed that six hundred years of English history make

the interpretation of the written word difficult. From the oldest to the most recent writings of the Bible is a span of about one thousand years, the distance between us and Alfred the Great. Two languages (three in fact, but Aramaic is found on only a few pages) appear in the Bible; we are dealing not with one but with two language communities. And the individual person is inserted into the language community only at his point in time; when he studies other points in time, he is to a greater or lesser degree a tourist in a foreign land.

The point to which this consideration, perhaps digressive, leads is the point that when God is said to have written the Bible, it is implied that he became a member of the Israelite and the Roman-Hellenistic language communities. The analogy of the Incarnation returns to mind; when Jesus was born he became a member of the Palestinian Jewish community. But to extend the analogy to the point where we say that the language of God was Hebrew, a dialect of Canaanite, the mind boggles a bit. The human authors were members of linguistic communities; it is not necessary that God also became a member of those communities. But God writes with the resources and the limitations of those linguistic communities, and like all authors he loses something in translation.

To the belief that the Bible is the word of God must be added the recognition that the Bible did not arise in a literary culture. The entire Bible was written in times and places in which all but a few of the population could not read. Before the invention of printing in the fifteenth century of our era written works could be reproduced and distributed only in handwritten copies, which were of necessity very few. It is difficult for the modern reader to grasp that in biblical times writing was really not a means of publication as we under-

stand it. Greek and Roman writers presented their works to a
limited public by reading them aloud, or by hiring a professional to read them aloud. The late W. F. Albright used to say
that in the ancient world writing was merely a record of the
spoken word and not a word in itself, as it is with us.

This may suggest that the men of the biblical world, who
did not think of the biblical works as the word of God, did not
attach the importance to the written word which we do. They
did not think of the inspired book or the inspired writer,
precisely the places where our problems are found. They did
think of an inspired speaker, the man to whom the word of
the Lord came; and the record of what he said would have
been the record of inspired speech. If the idea of inspiration
were pursued along these lines, the inquiry would take a
different form from the form it has taken in theology. But
theological tradition would not permit the pursuit of this line.
It would indeed deal with the inspired words of the prophets,
but not with the writings of the scribes who wrote narratives or
hymns or wise sayings. None of these pretended to have
prophetic inspiration nor were thought to have it by others. If
Paul thought of himself as an inspired writer, he was remarkably successful in concealing this idea.

In the apostolic church the gospel, the "good news," was
"proclaimed," "announced," "preached," as Jesus himself
had proclaimed the good news that the reign of God was at
hand. The proclamation imposed upon the hearer the choice
of belief and repentance. I say imposed the choice, not belief
itself; one who had heard the proclamation might not believe,
but it was because he had refused to believe, not because he
had never had the choice. The proclamation left no room for
the "invincible ignorance" which modern theologians invoke
so often. In the apostolic church the proclamation of the

gospel set up a personal encounter, inescapable and inevitable. The proclamation rendered the living Christ present to the hearer. The apostles quoted Jesus as saying, "He who hears you hears me." The hearer heard the living, the risen Christ as personally and as surely as those who had heard him in Galilee and Judea.

In a non-literary culture the gospel could only be proclaimed by a living speaker to a living hearer. This is not to imply that the word of power of the gospel had anything corresponding to it in the Hellenistic world; neither did the prophetic word of the Lord have anything like it in the ancient Near East. Jewish rabbis were able to quote the entire Bible from memory; Christian scribes apparently had the same skill. Books were indeed known and used, but they were really useful only to those who had memorized their contents. We do not have this skill because our possession of the printed word makes it unnecessary. I merely mean to suggest some reasons why the ancient attitude toward the written word of God was not the same as ours. The apostles would never have believed that faith could come through reading.

A corollary of the belief that God wrote the Bible has long been that the Bible is the only book which is free of error. In modern times the more we have learned about the Bible the more anguish belief in inerrancy has caused students of the Bible. The belief was easier to maintain when nothing was known of the ancient world except what the Bible tells us, and when the natural sciences had not disclosed knowledge of nature which went beyond the simple observations of the naked eye. It has long been obvious that the biblical writers knew no more about nature and history than any of their contemporaries; yet the devout felt an obligation to explain these limitations as something else than error. We know that

Belshazzar was not the son of Nebuchadnezzar, and that Darius the Mede, who succeeded him, is a nonexistent person. For no other writer would we feel compelled to say that not the author but his sources were in error. Is it too much to ask that an infallible writer should correct his sources? The Gospel of Matthew (27:9) once quotes the book of Zechariah under the name of Jeremiah. Were I to do this, both I and those who read or heard me would know that it was a lapse of memory. But God's memory does not lapse; hence exegetical literature has been forced to waste its time explaining that the text used by the author of Matthew did not distinguish the book of Zechariah from the book of Jeremiah—thus causing a confusion which occurs nowhere else in Jewish or Christian literature.

To return to the analogy of the Incarnation, such contrived explanations have suggested to modern theologians that just as the Word assumed a body subject to illness, injury and death, so God inspired writers who had all the weaknesses of writers. One of these is error. And no one should think that the Bible is free from error; I have given only two of a number of examples which no one to my knowledge has taken the trouble to count. One who affirms the total inerrancy of the Bible has the task of explaining these phenomena in some other way than the way he would use for any other book or article. It is a challenge which he ought to pause before accepting.

It is a modern but now somewhat antiquated defense of the Bible to say that it is an inerrant guide in religious matters but not in secular knowledge. And this is the way Christians have always looked at it. For the Jewish scribes from pre-Christian times to modern times the Bible contained all the knowledge which God wished man to have, and the learning of the Gentiles was folly. But even in this restricted sense the thesis is not tenable. Catholics can no more have an infallible Pope than Protestants can have an infallible Bible; one is committed to both but not assured of infallibility. Modern Catholics are learning to live with an infallible teacher who occasionally makes mistakes. They must also live with an inerrant Bible which quotes Zechariah as Jeremiah. They must also live with a Bible which proposes religious proposi- tions which they do not accept. I am not thinking of Jesus' words on nonviolence, to which we pay lip service, saying that we regret that it is impossible to live the good life as Jesus described it. I have in mind the Old Testament ethic of the holy war and the book of Esther.

The theology is not found in any one book, but it is associated with the theology we call Deuteronomic. The theology and the story both make virtues of and invoke God's blessing upon a murderously vindictive hatred of enemies, both political and religious. In the name of the holy war Christians from the time when they were allowed to bear arms have killed people, sometimes each other, in various types of crusades. The book of Esther presents a Jewish dream in which the oppressed are able, at least this once, to get back at the oppressors. What they did to their enemies in the book of Esther is, to risk giving offense without caring a lot, what Hitler did to Jews in as much of western Europe as he could reach. The book of Esther is so hard to "teach" without raising more problems than the teacher can solve that teachers leave it alone.

It may seem that I have dealt with more problems about biblical inspiration than I have presented easy, comfortable answers. If I have, I have been faithful to the situation. There are many problems in this area, and at the moment, as I said at the beginning, theologians seem to feel helpless before them. The reader who begins to feel concern about this belief should know that he has much company.

# 2

## IN THE BEGINNING GOD MADE

THE account of creation stands at the beginning of the Bible, and Bible readers would say that is just where it ought to stand. The first words of the Bible are, "In the beginning." The beginning is absolute; before God creates nothing exists besides himself. What he creates is heaven and earth. The enumeration of the major elements of heaven and earth follows through eight works distributed over six days; and at the end of the six days God enters into an eternal Sabbath rest. Creation is done. Living beings which are capable of reproducing their species have been established, and they live in a universe which is equipped with the elements necessary to sustain life. The enumeration indeed appears by modern standards to include a very small universe, not at all the universe as modern science views it. If it is diagrammed, it will show the earth as a flat disk floating in water, covered by the inverted bowl of the sky. But the existence of interstellar distances and stars of greater magnitude than the sun and galaxies of millions of suns do not postulate another creator.

The presence of the creation account at the beginning of the Bible gives it a certain controlling position which has obscured the fact that it is only one of several views of creation. In modern times the discovery of ancient Near Eastern creation myths has made it imperative that we recognize these other views, now that their antecedents are known. The same myths make it possible for us to understand the emphasis in Genesis I on only one creator with no helper, and the once-for-all creative action which is followed by the Sab-

19

bath rest, the cessation of creative activity. The other myths show us that the account of Genesis I is important less for what it says than for what it does not say.

In the myths which scholars have recovered there is a certain recurring pattern of creation. In all except Egyptian myths creation is the result of a victorious combat. The adversaries in this combat are the creative deity and an enemy who represents chaos. The enemy really has no form (chaos by definition), but appears as a monster, a dragon, a serpent of cosmic dimensions. In one Mesopotamian myth it is clearly female, but not too much should be made of this. Ancient mythology has no myth of the origin of sex except the Israelite myth, to which we shall come later. To other peoples sexual differentiation was not a thing to be explained.

In such a conflict of opposing principles.we have an example of that mythological idea which is called dualism. The two principles may be called light and darkness, order and chaos, good and evil. In dualism the opposition of the two is what sustains reality. The life of the world is the result of tension. The tension between the two poles is morally neutral, and "good" and "evil" become inappropriate terms for them. Neither pole can exist without its opposite. The ancients knew that nature is cyclical, with recurring patterns of seasons and of life and death. Let us for the moment leave ethical thinking out of this, and merely note that a view that the structure is sustained by tension between opposites is likely to lead to the idea that society is sustained by a similar tension between opposites. I use, of course, the language of abstract thought to set this forth; the ancients told a story of a conflict between Marduk and Tiamat or between Aleyan Baal and Mot.

The question now arises whether, since it is tension which sustains the universe, the myths of creation were myths of origin or myths which made it possible to live in a world sustained by tension. One observes that the place of the Mesopotamian myth of creation was in the New Year festival, which re-enacted ritually the death-life cycle of fertility. Jesus was quoted as saying that a seed produces no fruit unless it dies (John 12:24). This is hardly accurate by modern standards, but it is another expression of the ancient recognition of the life-death cycle, the tension of opposites.

From life comes death and from death life. Thus we conclude (as not all scholars do) that the creation celebrated in the Mesopotamian New Year was not an absolute beginning but an annual event. Each year the creative deity must conquer anew the adversary who is never totally and finally defeated. There is no myth of origin because the peoples of Mesopotamia and Canaan did not think of a time when the universe did not exist. It was always there because the principles of tension were always there; one could not imagine them beginning.

The student of the Bible must recognize that the creation account of Genesis I did not have in Israelite belief the controlling position which it has in Christian tradition. Critical scholars attribute the document to that biblical source known as the Priestly Document (P), which is post-exilic (later than 540 B.C.). It is possible that P contains material older than the date of its collection; but there are reasons for thinking that the creation account is not much earlier than 540 B.C., if it is indeed earlier at all. As we have observed, it is only one view of the creation myth—and this is the word we must use. The other views appear only in fragments, not woven into a

continuous narrative like Genesis I. We have observed that
other ancient myths enable use to recognize in these fragments a myth of combat and victory.

God divided the sea, broke the heads of the dragons,
crushed the heads of Leviathan (Psalm 74:13-14). The name
Leviathan is now known as the name of a mythological
monster of chaos in the Canaanite mythology or Ugarit. God
rules the raging of the sea, stills its waves, crushed Rahab,
made the heavens, the earth and the world (Psalm 89:9-11).
He punishes Leviathan the fleeing serpent and Leviathan the
twisting serpent with his great, hard and strong sword and
slays the dragon in the midst of the sea (Isaiah 27:1). This is
almost a verbal quotation from a Canaanite mythological
poem which we have in a copy seven to eight hundred years
earlier than the Judahite author; and we know that the site
where the texts were found was destroyed and permanently
abandoned about 1200 B.C.

One must suppose that the poem was widely circulated,
and perhaps the line had become a commonplace. God cut
Rahab in pieces, pierced the dragon, dried up the sea, the
waters of the great deep (Isaiah 5:9-10). The helpers of
Rahab bowed beneath God (Job 9:13). God stilled the sea
and smote Rahab. By his wind the heavens were made fair
and his hand smote the fleeing serpent (Job 26:12-13). He
shut in the sea with doors, clothed it with clouds and darkness, set bounds, bars and doors for it, and addressed it,
forbidding it to go any farther (Job 38:8-11).

We can remark several things about these passages. There
are clear allusions to a combat and a victory, and the victory
issues in creation. The identity of the adversaries remains
vague; Rahab, for example, is found nowhere in ancient
mythology nor elsewhere in the Bible (except Isaiah 30:7,

which seems to be a reference to an inactive monster). There is no way of distinguishing even fragments of this myth of a combat and victory from what appears to be the common Near Eastern myth of creation. The Israelites certainly knew this myth. It appears that they did not immediately see the consequences of the dualistic view of the world, the consequences being that God was not really supreme. Scholars now generally agree that creation as an act in the absolute beginning first appears in Second Isaiah (about 550 B.C.). In earlier Israel it appears that the common myth was uncritically accepted, and very probably that it was accepted as an annually recurring event.

It should be observed that the myth of creation as a view of reality sustained by perpetual tension appears to be a much more rational view of the universe than the biblical and Christian assertion of God's absolute supremacy. God's supremacy is not a fact of experience; the facts of experience present evidence which has been marshaled against God's supremacy. The myth accepts the things which we call evil as constituent principles of reality. It enables man to live with them by giving him the assurance that the monster, living and active, never wins a total victory, just as it is never totally defeated. Man can and does live with the tension.

More reflection was necessary to see that a God who is not supreme does not deserve trust and confidence. Ultimately he cannot save, for neither does he ever achieve a lasting victory. Even the modern believer, who thinks he is much more sophisticated in his faith than the ancient Israelites, has difficulties affirming God's supremacy in a world in which God seems less concerned with asserting his supremacy than we are. Yet the acquiescence with evil which the myth recommends is ultimately a denial that there is a power greater than ourselves. The Israelite scribes, as all believers must, found this an affirmation that reality is in the last analysis irrational, "a tale told by an idiot, full of sound and fury, signifying nothing."

The first step in preserving the rationality of being was to historicize the myth. The mythological event differs from the historical event precisely in that it is not an event; it is an enduring reality of some kind, a condition of being, a recurring phenomenon, which is derived from an archetypal event. The archetypal event endures and is encountered each time the condition or the phenomenon is experienced. Second Isaiah historicized the event and made it a once-for-all unique event. He did not, we have seen in the quotations above, remove the image of the victorious combat. And the event retained a certain archetypal quality; for he who created the world will by the same power do a greater work in the creation of his people anew after they have been historically annihilated. No adversary can stand against the victorious creator God; the idea of combat was not repugnant to his faith in God, but the idea of a perpetual unresolved combat was.

The scribe of Genesis I did find the idea of a combat repugnant. He rewrote the myth in such a way as to remove the combat—and with it the victory. But where there is no real adversary relation the word "victory" can be no more than a feeble figure of speech. Since there is no perpetual tension in a world in which God is absolutely supreme, creation was not and could not be a recurring event. All that God made was good, which really says more than that God made no evil; it also says that what God made is beyond improvement. The scribe historicized the myth into a single unique event more explicitly than Second Isaiah did. The Sabbath rest of God

not only denies further improvement; it also denies any necessity for God to protect his work from any adversary.

I said that the scribe rewrote the myth. One did not respond
in his world to myth by adducing arguments from philosophy
and theology; one responded to one story by telling another
story. That the scribe was responding to the common creation
myth has now become abundantly clear; it shaped his imagination and his thinking. The chaos monster, it seems, appears
in the creation account; it is probably the *tohu wabahu,* the
"void and empty" or "desolation and waste" of the English
versions. If it is, it has been deprived of personality and
power. It is there—the scribe was not thinking of creation
from nothing. It lurks in darkness, but the darkness has not
the demonic character of mythological darkness. Yet it must
be dispelled by God's creation of light. Light is the element
proper to deity, as darkness is the element of the monster of
chaos; the themes remain, but there is no conflict. But it takes
little knowledge of mythology to see that the light which is the
first work of creation is not the light which comes from the sun
and moon and other celestial luminaries.

In the course of the works of the six days God is said both to
"make" and to produce by a creative word of command. For
some works both phrases are used. Interpreters have thought
that the scribe mixed two views of the creative action. Creation by word seems to reflect a less primitive and more
elevated view of the creative activity, and indeed it may; but it
is not original with the biblical writers. It is found in an
Egyptian creation theology which probably goes back to the
third millennium B.C. We have already remarked that the
Egyptian creation myths do not exhibit the myth of conflict.

There is a wide consensus among modern interpreters that
the Genesis I creation account was written as a polemic

against the common myth of creation which is found in Mesopotamian and Canaaite sources. It is also commonly said that some form of these Mesopotamian or Canaanite myths was the object of the polemic. It does not appear that we need go so far afield to find the myth which, as we said, shaped the scribe's imagery and thought. We have ample evidence cited above that there were Israelite forms of the myth of the creative combat. It is true that we know these only in fragments, but they tell us enough to suggest that the scribe was concerned not with foreign myths but with Israelite myths. The myth, we said, was not an effort to explain the origin of the universe; it was an effort to make it possible for man to live in the universe as he experiences it. Other ancient Near Eastern peoples appear to have found some satisfaction in resigning themselves to an eternal tension between opposing poles of power. Neither power was really "friendly"; man could survive with some peace of mind only by adjusting his way of life and his ideals and his desires to inexorable reality.

At least some Israelites could not yield to cosmic despair. As we have suggested, they could not commit themselves to a God who was engaged in an eternal wrestling match. But when we talk in these terms, we are not attending to the question of how the world came to exist. Even the once-for-all creation of Genesis I bases its imagery and thinking on the cosmic myth; we have said before and must repeat that it historicizes the mythical event. This is not all it does; the modifications introduced into the myth of the creative combat are substantial. But the account shows no knowledge of the event of creation which is not derived from the myth of the creative combat.

Much ink and energy have been wasted since the middle of the nineteenth century concerning the reconciliation of the creation account with modern science. Early practitioners of the earth sciences, or some of them, affirmed that the Bible contained gross and childish errors concerning the origin of the universe. Believers in response affirmed that the inerrant Bible gave an account of the origins of the universe to which the sciences had better accommodate themselves. This dispute seems to be long dead, but it was ended on terms not entirely satisfactory. In the popular mind the scientists won the debate and left the impression that the Bible is not to be trusted as a source of information on the origins of the universe. Some concluded that it is no more to be trusted on other matters.

It may seem to be an evasion to insist that the Bible should be judged on what it says and means, not on its failure not to say what it does not mean to say. I have remarked several times above that the creation myths are attempts to explain how men should live in the existing world, not explanations of how the world came to exist. If the question were put in this way, the common myth would answer that it never came to exist; it is always there and it is recreated each year. Second Isaiah would answer that it was created by God; I doubt that he meant that the stars marching out each evening as God calls their names is to be taken as anything else but imagination. They had no experience of the event of creation, certainly, and if one alleges that they had divine revelation describing it, it is odd that God revealed only in terms of the common creation myth.

The controversy concerning the origins of the world was a replay of the Galileo controversy of the early seventeenth century with a different cast of characters. The theologians of the nineteenth century seemed to have learned nothing from the embarrassment of their predecessors. I am not sure that even yet the principle is established that the Bible neither asks nor answers scientific questions. This principle does not settle everything without further questions; and of these the first is what is a scientific question. As a preliminary we may say it is a question which science equips one to ask and to answer. I suggest that the questions whether God created the universe is one which science equips neither to ask nor to answer. Theologians do fear that if the question is put in the terms of what science can and cannot do, the direction of modern thought is to make the methods of the natural sciences the only valid methods of knowledge. One may ask whether the theologians fear that the scientists will do what theologians did in the Galileo case.

Let us return to what I said earlier, that the ancient mythographers had no experience of the event of creation. In fairness to the mythographers as well as to modern theologians it should be observed that neither do the natural sciences speak of creation from experience. They have drawn conclusions from the present condition of the universe to the processes by which it arrived at its present condition. One has no reason to question the careful and critical methods of investigation and deduction. These methods, like other scientific methods, can be criticized only by those who are trained in them. The conclusions reached are, like myth, symbolic expressions of a reality which is not known by experience; I owe this phrase to the late Ernest Cassirer. As hypothetical conclusions they are open to further modifications either because of new evidence or by improvement in the techniques of observation and deduction.

However, one can be nearly absolutely certain that the modifications will not present a process of eight works in six days. Among other things the ancient mythographers were unacquainted with that immanent force of change in nature which goes under the vague and general name of evolution. Whether in the common myth or the Genesis myth, the process of creation issues in a fixed world, the world of experience. It is not fixed; evolution has not come to a halt. But it is fixed enough to furnish a stable base for the course of several generations of human life, and that is as far as the interest of most men has ever reached.

When the believer professes his faith that creation is the work of a God who is absolutely supreme, he has said all that his faith has entitled him to say. Further questions about the process of origin in detail are scientific, and faith antecedently places no limit to the questions. We do not foresee any way in which by scientific method it can be proved that God "created" the universe, whatever we may mean by the term; in the same way, we do not foresee any way in which by scientific method it can be proved that God has nothing to do with it.

## UP FROM THE APES

HOW man came to be lies outside the frontiers of human knowledge and it does not seem likely that these frontiers will be pushed back in our lifetime. The title chosen for this chapter makes an obvious reference to the hypothesis of the evolution of higher forms of life from lower forms, the hypothesis which has dominated scientific and popular thinking on man and his origins for over a century. This hypothesis will not be discussed here for the good reason that the author pretends to no competence in the natural sciences; it ought to be said, and perhaps no more need be said, that the competence of scholars deserves as much respect here as elsewhere.

For much of the last hundred years many theologians believed that biblical evidence demanded that the hypothesis of evolution be rejected. We no longer understand the Bible as they did and cannot employ it in disputes about the evaluation of scientific evidence. It may also be said that the farther back examination goes into human prehistory—for human history is a mere five thousand years—the more uncertain the tracing of the steps of human evolution becomes. The origin of man, by which I mean the first appearance of the human species, still lies outside the frontiers of human knowledge.

The mistake of our theological predecessors was to think that the Bible delivered knowledge on this topic which was not available to scientific methods. We know now that for the biblical writers, as for their contemporaries in the ancient world and for modern scholars, the main evidence for any explanation of how man came to be is what man is. Certainly the modern scholar has a much wider vision of the human experience than the scribes of the ancient Near East. These scribes dealt with myth. While it is tempting to take up the rest of this chapter and perhaps more with a theoretical explanation of myth—and might be more profitable than what I intend to do—I believe that a basic understanding can be communicated without entering into a long discussion in technical language.

We all know myths and use them, often without recognizing them as such. Once we learn to identify them, it is not hard to look for their meaning. Myth is an attempt to enable man to live with certian phenomena by reducing them to some primordial event which is understood as enduring or recurring in the world of experience. To say that you cannot fight City Hall implies a myth of City Hall which so many people accept that the myth, so to speak, validates itself. Of course you can fight City Hall, you can even win the fight; but your victory will be achieved only by destroying one myth and replacing it with another.

The myth of the origins of man describes an event or a series of events which produce man in the terms in which the myth-making culture understands man. A myth of an enduring event which endures in the Australian Bushmen may enable the Bushman to live with himself; it will not do the same thing for the urban dweller in a commercial and industrial complex. Unfortunately the urban dweller is not as explicit in the mythology of origin as the Bushman; and this may be one of the reasons why he suffers from *anomie* or alienation, which do not trouble the Bushman until he is embraced by civilization. I observe that the purpose of the myth is not to explain reality but to enable men to live with it.

It is a long-standing mistake in biblical interpretation to take the narrative of Genesis 2 as the controlling pattern; it was done because this chapter (and the one following) was thought to be the account of an event just as it happened, an event of which the only witness could be the agent, God himself. It was not recognized that biblical scribes could themselves attempt to explain the human phenomenon by constructing a myth of origin. Man was produced by God because the biblical scribes had no idea of anything produced without God.

The author of Genesis 2 described man as a mud doll which gets up and walks and talks when God breathes into its nostrils. The breath of God is life. Let us not think of the soul, a product of Greek philosophical thought some centuries later. When God takes away his breath, as the biblical writer Koheleth said, man dies, and the breath returns to God (Ecclesiastes 12:7). Man is made of mud, obviously, because that is what the doll returns to when it loses its breath. But while the doll lives with the breath of God it is called not mud but flesh, a component which man shares with animals. Because man is flesh he is mortal, his physical strength is limited, and his moral strength as well. It is this component which elicits God's pity for him (Genesis 6:3). It is the root, to anticipate a phrase from Paul, of sin and death.

This seems to fulfill the definition of myth as the description of man's origin in terms of what man is observed to be. We have to turn to another myth found in Genesis I for an additional insight: that man is made in the image and likeness of God. Naturally since the Jewish rabbis began to discuss the Bible there has been deep theological interest in this line; and some conclusions have been drawn which were hardly in the mind of the author. One is tempted to think of the Second

Commandment—known to this scribe—and to say that God prohibited making an image of himself because he had already made the exhaustive image of himself; this would not be much more fanciful than some interpretations of this verse, and those who like such fancies may play with this one.

In the context of the creation story the line clearly affirms a dignity of man, the climax of God's creative works, which is not affirmed of anything else. Some interpreters have said that the image consists in man's dominion over the other works of creation; whether this is the image or not, man certainly is given dominion, and in another mythical image dominion is conferred in the myth of Genesis 2. But the image does not appear in this nor in the following chapter; that man is flesh is emphasized, and precisely the weakness of the flesh. This will come up again in our discussion. With the image and likeness of God may be associated the saying of Psalm 8:5, that you have made a little less than God (RSV) and crowned him with glory and honor, and set him over the works of your hands.

Man's rule over animals again illustrates that mythological thinking; a recognized feature of the human condition is attributed to a commission from God. In Genesis 2 there is a certain kinship between man and the animals; in fact the myth treats the animals as failed efforts to produce another creature like man. They are not worthy of him, and this is shown by the conferring of names upon them. Man can name them, but they cannot name him. In ancient law and custom to confer a name was an act of ownership. The kinship mentioned should not be pushed by the "pathetic fallacy" which has become so common in the modern world. Simpler cultures use animals with no guilt feelings. When I was much younger my elders told me that it was said on the farm, "If you are going to eat it, don't name it." The ancient Israelites would hardly have understood the modern mythology of animals; they would have understood that to give an animal a personal name is to admit it into the family. There is some inconsistency in slaughtering animals by the millions for food and at the same time supporting at no small cost organizations which are dedicated to the abolition of hunting, the fur trade and prevention of cruelty to pets. This the ancient Israelites would surely not have understood.

Yet it is part of the mythology of the priestly writer that earliest man did not eat animals. Man was a vegetarian until after the deluge, when God gave him the right to eat meat— again the myth which endures in reality. Does this imply that the eating of meat is a sign of moral degeneration? Hardly; the priestly scribe did not think of God as authorizing a moral degeneration. This saying is not a restriction of man's dominion over animals.

Man's relation to the lower animals was not the major point of the myth either of Genesis I or of Genesis 2. The major point of Genesis 2 was not the creation of the world, which is merely summarized, nor the creation of the animals, but the origin of two sexes. This was not unimportant to the scribe of Genesis I; besides his statement that man is made in the image and likeness of God, he says explicitly that God made them (men) male and female. Most interpreters have seen in this emphasis a statement that sex was instituted by creation and was not found on the level of divinity itself, as it was represented in ancient mythological polytheism.

The scribe thus removes sex from God himself; and it is probably a defect of grammar and vocabulary that God is mentioned as a masculine noun which takes masculine adjectives, pronouns and verbs. There was simply no way in the resources of language to speak of a personal being who transcended gender. The use of the feminine would certainly have had implications which the scribe did not wish; and Hebrew grammar lacks the neuter form. There is no myth of the origin of the sexes in Mesopotamia, Egypt or Canaan. This point deserves some attention only because of certain unfounded theological conclusions which have been drawn because the God of the Old Testament is grammatically masculine.

In Genesis I the creation of man is clearly climactic in the creation myth. Genesis 2 has a different order of material: creation by the irrigation of the desert, the creation of the human male, the creation of a place for him to live, the creation of the animals as experiments to furnish a companion for the man, and the creation of a woman from the body of the male (and not from clay). The creation of the woman is just as obviously climactic as the creation of man in Genesis I.

The appearance of the woman evokes a solemn declaration which deserves some study. We saw above that the conferring of a name is an act of ownership. The man confers the name on the woman and by giving the name denies his ownership. The saying recognizes that she is not like the animals which he has named but is like himself; and her name (by a rather questionable Hebrew etymology) designates that she stands with the male on a different level from the animals. She is what God sought and found almost by trial and error, the helper fit for the man (RSV), the one with whom he can become one flesh. One should not lean too heavily on the word "helper" in defining the relations of the two sexes; the same word is used of God when he is invoked as helper, and the psalmist scarcely intended to summon God as his assistant.

It has long seemed to me that this episode initiates a human social relation which is entirely free of any suggestion of domination. This is significant, because the author lived in a culture of male domination which went back to the beginning of time, as far as any one knew. The world had to wait for Greek philosophy to deliver rational arguments about the intellectual and biological inferiority of women; and some of the later wise men of the Bible were rather candid about their moral inferiority.

In the ancient Near Eastern cultures of which the scribe was a contemporary the social depression of women was lived as a simple fact of life, neither defended nor criticized. In such a world one would not expect the scribe to mount a full frontal assault on the prevailing and unquestioned social system. Even the Ten Commandments include the wife with other property in the prohibition of coveting another's property. Perhaps the scribe thought he could do no more than compose or reinterpret a myth which said that the social system was not as God had made it. If the reader will stay with this book, he or she may see how this view is confirmed by the fuller development of the story of Eden. But even without the sequel, it seems that the story of the creation of woman asserts the equality of the two human beings. Until woman is created, the creation of man is an unfinished job.

It is not without interest that in the myth of origin of Genesis 2 man does not appear as a social being. He probably does so appear in Genesis I; nothing in the text indicates that a single couple is meant, and other myths of human origins generally describe the origin of a human community. They recognize that man in fact cannot survive except as a community; and we have to ask why the myth of Genesis 2 deviates from what appears to be the common pattern. We shall have to touch upon this again; but it appears that for this scribe the origin of the human community is associated with the rise and spread of sin. The original couple lives in an oasis in the midst of a cosmic desert; this desert is empty for the purposes of the writer. They are fortunate peasants; the man is said to till the soil, but the subsequent development of the myth makes it clear that this is no burden. They live in a world in which there is no disturbing element.

It has long been noticed that the story of a fall from grace has left no influence in the books of the Old Testament; it is not picked up by any biblical writer before Paul. But the idea of a peaceful paradise of bliss left many echoes; it is the consummation which human history is destined to restore. The last act of salvation is a restoration of the beginnings. The author of Isaiah 11:6-9 added a feature which does not appear in Genesis 2 when he introduced into the eschatological paradise the theme of peace even in the animal world; beasts will no longer prey on one another. He was, however, faithful to the spirit of the scribe of Genesis 2. God could not and did not make a world in which disturbing elements were constitutive; and one may ask what the disturbing elements may be.

In fact the scribe does admit one element which could be called disturbing, and that is the element of challenge. Man must do something—rather abstain from something—in order to maintain himself in a paradise of bliss. This challenge, with its implicit possibility of disturbance, was forced upon the scribe by the fact that man does not live in a paradise of bliss. It was his purpose in the subsequent development of the myth to show how this came about; and his mythology is less than logical in admitting the possibility of disorder. How did the serpent get into the garden? The scribe never tells us because he could not explain it.

There is an ancient interpretation of the myth of paradise,

accepted by the second century church father Irenaeus, among others, that the paradise of bliss represents the couple as having the innocence of children; and this idea is somewhat supported by their unashamed nudity. It follows therefore that their sin was to grow up. We now recognize that the couple are not historical persons like David and Bathsheba, that they are very probably typical figures of Man and Woman. When we discuss the myth of the fall in Genesis 3, we shall see that what the scribe attaches to the fall as its consequences is not easily associated with the simple fact of growing into maturity. Yet it is not without interest that Jesus himself described belief in him as becoming like little children.

There is no reason to think that the scribe did not draw upon the only human innocence we know, the innocence of childhood, for the traits of Man and Woman in paradise. The innocent and well-protected child lives without fear or responsibility; if the peoples of the ancient Near East were like their modern successors in the same regions, they went to great trouble to preserve their children innocent from fear as long as possible. Something irreplaceable is lost when childhood innocence is lost; but the business of the world could not be conducted unless it were lost. Perhaps this among other things is what the myth wanted to say. The business of the world is conducted at a very great price, perhaps greater than we know. When God made Man and Woman, they had no business of the world to conduct.

One very important derivation from the myth of the paradise of bliss was the theological doctrine of what was called by Thomas Aquinas the state of original justice. Thomas Aquinas and his contemporaries never thought of the story of Eden as anything other than sober history. They recognized that the history omits many details; but the use of reasoned imagination enables the theologian to supply the details which the history did not mention. The history implies that what I have called the human condition was not the condition in which God created man. God must have created man as the perfect human being. What, then, would be the perfect human condition for the perfect human beings?

Obviously the major threat to humanity is death; and the narrative says clearly that the couple is protected from the danger of death. The narrative is not clear on how this protection was achieved; apparently the fruit of the tree of life, when eaten regularly, warded off death. Man did not possess freedom from death as a permanent holding; it could be and was lost. But the perfect man should be spared the uncertainty of death.

Neither therefore could the perfect man be subject to other features of the human condition which endanger life; and the first of these are the dangers to health. Most people die of illness; the perfect man must enjoy perfect health. Theoretically, if infection could get into paradise, the constitution of the perfect man would reject it. He must have absolutely perfect physical strength; and this carries with it grace and beauty of body.

The theological Adam and Eve were the strongest and the most beautiful people whom God ever made. And since people die of old age if nothing else, they could not grow old. This created something of a problem, for it is not only a biblical but a widely held human belief that wisdom came with age. It need not, for God can supply wisdom without the experience which produces it in the human condition we know—the knowledge of good and evil. So the theological Adam and Eve were not only strong and beautiful; they were also supremely wise and intelligent. And since wisdom is impossible unless one is master of one's desires, the perfect man was subject to no feeling which he did not dominate. The theologians felt that God would have created a moral cripple if he had created the man of experience, constantly driven by impulses which he controls with difficulty when he does control them.

So by what seemed to be quite sure theological reasoning the theologians created another myth to supplement— perhaps more to replace—the biblical myth of Genesis. Man must have been created in that condition which medieval theologians thought was the ideal human condition. Thomas Aquinas so described the perfection of Adam and Eve that he effectively made it impossible for them to make an error of judgment and to commit sin. The biblical myth more kindly and sympathetically suggests that they were simple and inexperienced children who got into trouble by not following clear and simple instructions, as children do. In the next chapter we shall see how the biblical presentation shows a growth in adult malice in the early generations of man. In the myth of Thomas Aquinas man has never since been as capable of adult malice as the theological Adam and Eve were.

# 4

## DOWN FROM THE ANGELS

GENESIS 3 is traditionally the story of the fall of man. We have noticed earlier that there is no clear allusion to this story elsewhere in the Hebrew Old Testament, not even in the chapters immediately following. In fact the theology of the fall leans more heavily upon Paul's epistle to the Romans (chapter 5), which is creative interpretation of a type well identified in rabbinical exegesis. Paul certainly took the chapter as historical; that he did so does not oblige us to follow him any more than his belief that the earth is flat is imposed upon us—a belief which several Christian teachers tried to impose. In both cases we have knowledge which Paul lacked, and we do not fault him for lacking it. The story is a myth, a word which we have used much; and we may recall that myth is an effort to explain existing reality by deriving reality from an event which is believed to endure or to recur in the present. We said that the myth of creation tries to explain how man came to be; the myth of Eden attempts to explain how humanity came to be what it is. It is not just human existence but the human condition which sets the problem.

The myth of a fall is not found everywhere in the world, nor is it even found often. The human condition is accepted rather than explained; it is not a problem, which means that man is thought to be no worse than he ought be. We observed that the myth of the fall is not echoed elsewhere in the Hebrew Old Testament. The earliest rationalist interpretation of the myth appears in a Jewish apocryphal book of the first century A.D., the Second Book of Baruch, in which the author wrote that each man is the Adam of his own soul. For the rest of the Old Testament, the question is whether the human condition, by which I mean the condition of sinfulness and mortality, is ever treated as anything but natural, in our sense of the word. This does not exclude occasional cries of anguish at the human condition, which are found in all literatures. Examples of such anguish can be found in the book of Job, the Psalms, and Ecclesiastes. Such outbursts of poetic lamentation are not serious questions about the human condition, as I believe this chapter is.

I said earlier that the position this chapter has had in Christian theology distorts its meaning somewhat. It has not often been noticed by readers and interpreters that Genesis 3-11 is a series of falls from virtue; and it may help if we recall them. There is Cain and the first murder; Lamech, the first polygamist and inventor of the blood feud; the wickedness of man which moved God to destroy man by a deluge; Noah, the first drunkard; Ham, the first homosexual; and Babel, the first effort to reach the level of God (distinguished from the Eden myth only because it is a collective effort).

Apart from some genealogical lists, which were inserted in the text by later authors and editors, the author either by coincidence or by design has collected a number of stories of paradigmatic sins. Each of them by itself could be the story of a fall. With the appearance of Abraham the author departs from the world of myth and enters the world of experience. One finds it difficult to believe that by mere coincidence the scribe selected only those myths which illustrate human sin. It is all the more difficult because the probability is that these myths were originally independent of each other; it was the scribe who wove them into a story of the growth of sin.

There is another factor involved in the fabric of the stories.

The story of sin is also the story of the growth of civilization. The first murderer is the builder of the first city. His descendant, Lamech, heads the family which invents stock-raising, music, and weapons. Noah, the inventor of viticulture, falls victim to the power of his own product. Babel, the first city (we said the author uses independent stories) is a challenge to God and results in the division of languages. The question has been asked by some interpreters whether the scribe was not expressing a somewhat veiled criticism of civilization and its arts. As he arranged his myths, the price of the development of civilization was man's moral integrity. Many readers have been reminded of Hosea 2:14, in which the regeneration of Israel must begin with a return to the desert, which means the abandonment of civilization and its comforts and arts. Even in the first of the scribe's "falls" he can describe the sin of the first pair no more precisely than as a search for knowledge. Knowledge of good and evil can mean in Hebrew knowledge of everything—not very probably; it can mean the desire to experience everything, and this is more likely.

By setting this context I wish to show that the scribe did not wish readers to think that his mythology of the human condition ended with Genesis 3:24. But it is the first in the series, and it gives a mythological answer to a number of questions, more than any other single myth in the series. Let us list them, without for the moment adverting to the fact that some are much more important than others: why people wear clothing; why snakes crawl; why people loathe and detest snakes; why women have pains in giving birth; why women are socially depressed; why the soil resists cultivation; why people die. This is an impressive list. Interpreters have often suspected that the scribe made one story out of several isolated myths, for each of these questions could stand with its story by itself. At the same time, it is not without interest that none of these questions are asked or answered in the ancient Near Eastern mythology which we know.

Most of these mythologies are so popular and naive that they need no discussion. All of these features of the human condition are the results of curses laid by God upon man and the world. The curse was an act of vengeance, an effective declaration that harm should be wrought. The myth does not accept sinfulness and mortality as constitutive elements of the human condition; they are intrusions, and they are due to the response of God to man's rebellion. The myth proposes, as clearly as myth can propose anything, that the human condition is the result of a decision made by man himself. It is not present because the world and man were so made, or because God acts capriciously, or simply because man is unlucky, the kind of cosmic loser which Greek tragedy made him out to be. Man is the way he is because he chooses to be that way.

This is the main thrust of the myth; the form of the writer's imagery raises other questions. We have asked one; how did the snake get into Eden? Obviously because God put him there; he was the most crafty of all the animals which God made. The ancient and venerable identification of the snake with the devil or Satan or whatever one chooses to call him is not accepted in modern theology; we shall have to discuss this more fully in another of these chapters. The student of ancient Near Eastern literature and art notices that in art the snake is often associated with the nude goddess of fertility. We believe this association would be as obvious to most ancient Israelites as it is to the modern orientalist. We can be no more precise than to say associated, because it is hard to define the symbolism of the snake with exactness. What we can say is that one symbol, the snake, evoked the other symbol, the image of the nude goddess. And so the woman has become a temptress because she has become what the Israelite abominated beyond all else, a false god.

This suggests that behind the simple childish pictures of a boy and a girl stealing fruit the Israelite could see the cult of fertility, the most widespread cult of the ancient world and the cult against which the Old Testament speaks more often than any other. One may say that the scribe told a myth which presented the fertility cult as the root of all our troubles. It might repay the serious reader, now that we have told him of the artistic symbolism of the snake, to go through the two chapters and count the obvious sexual allusions. It is because of these that one of the earliest interpretations of the myth saw it as symbolizing the loss of innocence through the discovery of sex, the process through which every normal adult passes. This interpretation, like the hundred-headed serpent of Greek myth, never quite dies; and what maintains it is the obvious sexual milieu of the scene of Eden. The curse of the woman falls precisely upon her sexual functions; the pains of childbirth and domination by the male. It may be imagined, although I recognize that it is rather fancy for an ancient mythographer, that the declaration of enmity between woman and the snake is a very early form of the modern saying that biology is destiny. If it is, the mythographer adds what the modern saying omits, that the biology which is destiny is a curse.

I drew attention earlier to the absence of any clear allusion to the social depression of women in the myth of the creation of man and woman. The curse of the woman makes it clear that the social depression of the woman begins here, just as the tilling of the soil become grinding labor instead of refreshing exercise. Man's world has been turned upside down; God does not destroy paradise, but he excludes man from dwelling there. And only there can man escape death. The subsequent history of the myth of a paradise still there but hidden from man's knowledge and approach is long and interesting, and perhaps we shall have occasion to pursue it in another of these chapters.

The reader is bound to ask, as so many have asked, what did the man and woman do? Eating forbidden fruit obviously is an image of something else; and I have remarked that the earliest explanation of the image as the enjoyment of sex has never died. It certainly survives in literature. I may interject that this view of sex is totally unbiblical, unless we are speaking of adultery. This cannot have been meant by the author; and if this seems an authoritative statement, let me say that I do no more than speak for the vast majority of modern interpreters. I may add that the Bible is entirely free of any Puritanical or Jansenistic view of sex. This comes from the heresy called Gnosticism and not from the Bible. If man is not in the Bible an ape on the make, neither is he a fallen angel. He is, as we have observed, flesh.

So if eating forbidden fruit does not mean the illicit use of sex, what does it mean? We interpreters have too often thought that the scribe was playing games with us; and it is true that the ancient wiseman did enjoy riddles. That riddle is best which has several answers. If this be such a riddle, the wiseman may smile and say that all your answers are right. On the other hand, he defined the sin only as a search for knowledge, using a term—knowledge of good and evil— which interpreters have found ambiguous. It was probably meant to be ambiguous, and in that sense the scribe does play games with us. It has no sexual overtones or undertones. Here to know most probably means to experience; and this is experience which is promised to make them like gods. To be like gods appears to mean ability to choose with no moral restraint except that which one imposes upon oneself. This may be subtle, but it is a mistake to think that this scribe was not subtle.

The late L.S.B. Leakey, one of the most distinguished African anthropologists of our time, discovered some fossil remains which not only suggested that man is much older than had been thought, but that his first sure signs of humanity were that he manufactured weapons with which he killed not only prey but his own species. Mr. Robert Ardrey, who has done much to popularize the research of Leakey and others, noticed that the first man is better called Cain than Adam.

The similarity between African anthropology and Genesis 4 is romantic, but it is the business of literary men and women to find romantic parallels. When the mythographer of Genesis gets to the first sin which he defines in unmistakable terms, it is the sin of murder. As we have remarked earlier, it is the children of Cain who build cities, devise skills by which natural resources may be exploited, and invent art and weapons. They also—and I mean this seriously—invent law and order. In the scribe's scheme they also reach a pitch of malice which makes God sorry he ever made them; the anthropomorphism is his, not mine.

I have remarked that in this collection we may have existing materials used and retreated; we cannot prove this because we do not have the other materials. In the story of the deluge we have several Mesopotamian versions of the myth, and we can see how the Israelite scribe rewrote the myth. The myths are all stories which begin with the anger of a god, his decision to destroy all mankind by a flood, the escape of one man and his family who is warned to build an "ark"—a strange floating house, or rather floating zoo. This survivor becomes the ancestor of all men. No one doubts that the Mesopotamian myth is the source of the biblical myths; the similarities are too close and too many, down to the use of birds to explore the presence of land.

The theological revisions of the Israelite scribe thus become clear. There is no reason for the anger of Enlil in the Mesopotamian myth; it is capricious. Mesopotamian man lived in a state of quiet terror because the powers which ruled his world were not reasonable. To those who identify the phenomena of nature with powerful personal wills it was accepted that a natural disaster was a manifestation of anger. We no longer look at nature in this way, and we do not ask why God was so angry in Guatemala and not here.

The Israelites did not believe that God was irrational or capricious, ready to say, "Off with his head!" like the Red Queen for a real or fancied slight, however minor. The scribe was careful to say that all flesh had corrupted its way and therefore deserved the capital sentence. Noah has retained his integrity and therefore ought to be spared. It is not clear that the scribe either saw or intended the implications that there was a new creation both of the world and of man. It is clear that the deluge of Genesis, unlike the deluge of Mesopotamia, was an act of justice and not of capricious anger. It expresses again the assertion that the human condition is the work of man's own choice.

One of the authors of the Mesopotamian myth makes the myth an organ of protest against the anger of the gods as seen in natural disasters. If the gods are angry at man for any reason serious or trivial, they ought to act with restraint in punishing. Enlil should have sent a wild beast or a disease, not a flood which destroys totally. This protest was not employed by the Israelite scribe because he did not question the justice of God. God punished in measure, and if the punishment was total it was proportionate to the offense. His implicit argument was the type we call *a priori;* if God did it, it must be morally irreproachable. He accepted the existence of natural disasters and he accepted them, as ancient man did, as the works of God's anger. It did not occur to him to rewrite the myth by denying that the deluge occurred. Nor did it occur to him, as it did occur to the Mesopotamian scribe, that the punishment was excessive. The same or another scribe faced the myth of the destruction of Sodom and Gomorrah by an unidentified natural disaster. If there were ten good men in the cities God should not inflict the punishment of total destruction. There were not ten, and the one family which, as immigrants, did not share in the moral guilt of the city, had to be removed by a messenger from God before the catastrophe could be inflicted and retain the quality of divine justice.

It may occur to the reader that these myths do indeed emphasize perhaps beyond need the theme of punishment of the guilty. Certainly a theology which sees all hostile elements in the universe as weapons of God's anger is an inadequate effort to attain some understanding of God. No one thinks that the entire revelation of the Bible is to be found in any simple passage or theme. It does not seem that the scribe's insistence that man is responsible for the human condition is a mythological image which may be treated like his image of the flat earth. One finds that the books of the Old Testament, as we have already indicated, treat man as a responsible agent, even when, like Ecclesiastes, some writers talk as if man were playing with a stacked deck.

The "fall" which followed the first creation is followed by

the strange "fall" of Noah and his son after the restoration. There are not many biblical references to intoxication, although the ancient world knew the problem and had words for it. In fact ancient methods of brewing and winemaking did not produce beverages of the explosive proof of modern intoxicants, and the ancient toper was likely to experience nausea before he reached the point of feeling no pain. This is represented in ancient Egyptian art. This is one of the few passages which speak with disapproval of intoxication; those who like to collect such passages may add Proverbs 23:29-35 (possibly the earliest use of the phrase "feel no pain" for intoxication) and Proverbs 31:4-7.

I remarked earlier that the sin of Ham is understood by most interpreters to refer to homosexuality. This is an educated guess, because there is no explicit mention of any specific action in the text. Nevertheless, there is not doubt of the general biblical repudiation of homosexual commerce, and the interpreters think they are doing no violence to the author when they read this into his mind. And it is likely that the scribe is more offended by the flagrant violation of filial piety than anything else.

The mythology of sin closes with the story of the tower of Babel. As we have remarked, this is a second account of the building of the first city; one does not search in myth for the kind of consistency which is sought in history. Scholars have often noticed indications here of the fusion of two originally distinct myths, but they have not been able to reconstruct to their satisfaction the two forms. As it stands, the myth explains the diversity of human languages. This diversity is taken as a symbol of human disunity. The two themes which scholars find are the building of the city and the building of the tower. The city is Babel, the Hebrew form of the Akkadian *babilu,* the name of the city we know as Babylon, which more than once appears in the Old Testament as the city which symbolizes wealth and power; indeed, it is used as an emblematic name of Rome in the New Testament. The name seems to have this emblematic value in the myth.

The tower is recognized as the Mesopotamian *ziggurat,* the freestanding tower which was erected adjacent to Mesopotamian temples. Its form and purpose are not well known, but it appears the scribe did not totally misunderstand it when he described it as a route of passage between heaven and earth. The same theme is suggested in the ladder of Jacob (Genesis 28). The scribe sees in this building an attempt to reach the dwelling of the gods; the theme somewhat echoes the theme of the sin of Genesis 3. The disunity of man, symbolized by the diversity of speech, becomes a part of the human condition. It is somewhat strange that in this whole series of the mythology of sin the scribe never speaks explicitly of what the Old Testament generally mentions as the basic and radical sin of man, the worship of false gods. We think it is suggested in Genesis 3, and the scribe certainly knew that his tower was a piece of cultic architecture. He never calls it that.

The effect of this series of myths, in spite of some loose features of organization, is powerful. It denies to man any escape from responsibility for the human condition. We are sure that the author had a broad acquaintance with ancient Near Eastern mythology, that he chose some myths and rejected others. What governed his choice becomes clear when the whole series is reviewed. Lacking history, ancient scribes dealt with the reality which lies beyond experience by mythology. It deserves to be treated seriously, not because we use myth ourselves—we do without knowing it—but because it is an important part of the human adventure and because it contains insights which are sometimes lost in the philosophy and science through which we attempt, to use again a phrase used previously, not to explain reality but to make it possible to live with reality.

# 5

## SPIRITS AND DEMONS

**I**T does not take a complete reading of the Bible to show that the writers of the Old and New Testaments and the people about whom they wrote lived in a world full of good spirits and bad spirits, angels and demons. The modern reader will have to confess that he or she does not live in such a world. Personally I have never encountered either an angel or a devil whom I could clearly identify as such, and I have never met a person who had a convincing experience of either. One may conclude from this with all due modesty that whatever directions one may deduce from the Bible on how to deal with angels and demons they have nothing to say to the world in which I live. This is not simple unbelief; I simply have never had to deal with such beings, and at my age I can hardly expect the problem to arise.

The more one knows about the world of the Bible the more clearly one sees that it would be most remarkable if the peoples of Israel and Judaism lived in a world which was free of good and bad spirits. Much of the demonology of ancient Mesopotamia passed through Greece and Rome into medieval Europe to survive into modern times. With the belief in demons passes much of the magic by which ancient man coped with demons. One prayed to the gods, but one evoked magic against demons.

It is not altogether true to say that the ancient world credited demons with any trouble which could not be rationally explained; but one can say that this is the direction in which thought moved. The ancient Mesopotamian who was pregnant lived surrounded by a host of demons who threatened her life and the life of her child. This is a more serious threat than a toothache or sour milk; the demons were more dangerous than *Poltergeister*. But they could not work catastropic disaster; this was the result of the anger of the gods.

Since so many human ills were the work of demons, the demons became specialized. It was necessary for the magician to know the demon against whom he should direct his incantation. The belief in the demons who haunted the pregnant reflects the high rate of infant mortality and of women in delivery. Rational medicine of a primitive kind was not unknown in ancient Mesopotamia, but it was unable to cope with disease. When one reads of some of the materials employed on the unfortunate patient in exorcising the demons, one sees that only a sturdy patient could survive.

Ancient artists have left us both word pictures and images of the monsters whom they feared. One recognizes some of the features of the devils of medieval Christianity; ultimately, there are only so many ways of depicting monsters, and they begin to resemble each other. Our friendly devils, like the one who used to be found on the label of Pluto water, are rather tame compared to the gargoyles of Chartres or Notre Dame, which hardly reward the stair climbing which one must do to view them. But they come out of the world of ancient Mesopotamia. They were intended to be repulsive; after all, they personified threats to human life and health.

But not all demons were bad in Mesopotamia. Man survived the attacks of demons because there were benevolent demons. The visitor to museums of ancient Near Eastern art is impressed by the gigantic figures with human heads on the bodies of bulls and lions. These demons protected the gates of temples and palaces. Obviously they did not protect them against hostile armies; they warded off hostile demons, and in some instances they are so ugly that it is hard to realize they are on our side.

Rationalism has never been enough to expel demons. We live in what we think is the age of Reason; those who think so should consider the reception given to the novel and the movie *The Exorcist*. But for the moment let us consider that civilization called Hellenism, which flourished from the fourth century B.C. to the fifth century A.D., more or less, from which much of western civilization is derived. The student of Hellenism sees the cult of reason carried to perhaps its peak. He sees also a whole culture dominating the Mediterranean which was so profoundly irreligious that it makes modern civilization look like the Age of Faith.

The peoples of the Hellenistic world, the learned and the unlearned, did not believe in God or gods; but they did believe in demons and magic. One may see something pathetic in the peoples of ancient Mesopotamia and the Hellenistic world, who created so much of what we still treasure as the world of civilization, sunk in gross superstition. Some fears they did not rationalize. I hope to point out shortly that their fears were reasonable but directed to the wrong object.

It is therefore worthy of notice that demonology plays a comparatively small part in the early books of the Old Testament; I mean the books which scholars believe are earlier than the Exile, effectively before 550 B.C. Early Israelite law severely prohibited the practice of magic, the biblical law which was responsible for the execution of witches in medieval and early modern Europe, and in Salem, Massachusetts, in 1692. Nothing of what we know in early Israel corresponds to the developed demonology of Mesopotamia.

It seems obvious that the early Israelites thought that demons were a rival power to God, and it was impossible to think of God having real rivals. These books of the Old Testament do not suggest that demons were much of a threat to the peace of mind of early Israel.

This does not mean that biblical language does not reflect demonology. Demons haunt abandoned ruins in some passages; this is probably no more serious than popular belief that ghosts haunt graveyards or houses in which violent death occurred. Some demons in ancient times were identified with the ghosts of the unburied or those who had been murdered by unknown hands. But demons in Mesopotamia were the spawn of the monster of chaos, who brought them forth to help her in her war against the creative deity of light. This is clear and unambiguous dualism.

This restraint did not endure in post-exilic Jewish literature. The best example of demonology in late Jewish literature is the book of Tobit or Tobias. The demon Asmodeus (probably derived from a Persian name of one of the seven evil spirits) infests Sarah as a jealous incubus who kills her seven husbands. He is expelled by the smoke of a burning liver of fish. One recognizes here ancient demonology and the magic ritual of exorcism.

Jewish belief in demons, however popular it might have been, would not tolerate the belief that demons came from the womb of the monster of chaos, nor the belief that a good God would create such evil beings. In extra-biblical late Jewish literature the theory was advanced that the demons were fallen angels; the fall is narrated in Genesis 6:1-6, the myth of the marriage of the sons of God with the daughters of men. I call this a myth because all my colleagues do, and it really can be nothing else. If one believes in the reality of demons, hardly any other rational explanation is possible. The question is concerned with the reality of demons. In most of the Old Testament, as we have remarked, demons are not regarded as a real threat to human welfare. When the belief is developed in Judaism, we can trace its roots in ancient superstition.

The Old Testament also knows good spirits. "The angel of the Lord" is a rare messenger of God, usually announcing a threat or a promise, but sometimes active. He always appears alone; and in most passages where he is mentioned he merges with God, for whom he speaks. Were he the only such appearance, interpreters would have no trouble in treating him as a personification of the word of God. But there are also passages which speak of the heavenly retinue of God; the host of heaven accompanies him, and with this host should be classed such beings as the cherubim and seraphim, which seem to suggest the hybrid benevolent demons, winged creatures combining human and animal features, which stood at the gates of Mesopotamian and Egyptian temples and palaces. Again, if these stood alone, they would be treated as personifications of the divine attributes. If God is imagined as a king, he must be given a court.

Like the demons, these heavenly beings are not prominent in the older books of the Old Testament. The early Israelite was not much afraid of demons, and he seems to have felt that God could do anything that a heavenly messenger could do; he did not expect much from the heavenly messengers. One later prophet (Isaiah 63:9, as translated in the Anchor Bible) wrote that in all their affliction it was no emissary nor messenger; it was his presence that saved them.

I realize that I have not presented all the evidence, and in this space I cannot present it, which shows that the world of angels and demons of the New Testament is the world of angels and demons of late Judaism. The New Testament lacks the restraint of the early books of the Old Testament. It is often argued that Jesus believed in angels and demons, and therefore we must. It seems simple, but it is not.

Jesus lived in patterns of thought and language which he did not invent and could depart from only at the cost of becoming unintelligible. His departures from customary patterns was so revolutionary that we have not grasped them, but they were not made at the cost of intelligibility. To love your neighbor as yourself and to treat your enemy as your neighbor is a more violent departure from customary patterns than to announce a heliocentric universe and a spherical earth. The New Testament accepts the common speech about angels and demons; it also announces a union of God with man that is not mediated by angels and proclaims a power which negates demonic power.

Angels are prominent in infancy narratives of Matthew and Luke and in the resurrection narratives, just those parts of the gospels which show most of that type of pious meditative expansion which is called midrash. The infancy and the resurrection narratives leave room for this type of expansion because there was no first-hand account of either series of episodes. In most of the incidents of the life of Jesus there was no room for the introductions of the angelic and demonic elements. Luke introduces angels into the life of the Jerusalem church, of which he had no personal experience. Paul mentions them as frequently as a rabbi might be expected to, but never as an object of personal experience. They become almost an element of literary ornamentation.

The demons become in the New Testament an agent of a kind of evil which first appears in late Judaism, and that is temptation to sin. The world of the New Testament was sufficiently rational to reject much of the antics attributed to demons in early Mesopotamia; but demons were blamed for much of the evil done by men. I shall point out below that this is an unjust evasion of responsibility. The temptations of Jesus, for instance, seem to have been written from the need to identify Jesus with the universal human experience of temptation. Since it could not have arisen in him from imperfectly controlled desires, it had to be the work of an external agent. Why not another man? Early Christians would have vomited out the suggestion that he could be tempted by a woman; that part of the human experience they refused to identify him with. The temptation narrative is symbolic, and seems to be addressed as much to the church as to Jesus; certainly the church has experienced all three temptations, and has fallen to all three.

What is to be said of diabolical possession? Do not the exorcisms of Jesus compel us to accept the reality of possession? One must again voice that the gospels were written in a world in which possession was an accepted phenomenon. In the time of my grandparents tomatoes were poisonous, in spite of the fact that no one ever died from eating them. One could not escape the language of the belief in possession without creating a new set of thought and language patterns. Jesus, I suppose, talked about these things in the way in which he talked about the flat earth sandwiched between heaven and hell. The fear of demons could have been removed by denying their reality no more easily than people were persuaded to eat tomatoes. In the gospels it is removed by the assertion that the demons are powerless before God.

Greek and Latin also exhibit forms of speech which attribute mental illness to foreign agents, sometimes indwelling demons. The word lunacy is derived from a Latin word meaning moon-sickness; the popular belief that the mentally disturbed suffer most at the full moon still survives. The Greek word mania suggests a supernaturally induced rage. It is not simply true that ailments of unknown causes were attributed to demons; but mental ailments usually were because they suggest a change of personality. Physicians say that the possessed boy in Mark 9:14-29 is almost a textbook case of epilepsy. Surely it is no less wonderful that God should have power over epilepsy than that he should have it over demons.

Such neat rationalism cannot so easily be applied to the maniac of Mark 5:1-20; and he too would be a textbook case were it not for the two thousand swine. Commentators therefore are inclined cautiously to treat the swine as an early Christian expansion which gives fuller meaning to the word "unclean" as applied to the evil spirits. But the problem is not resolved by the detailed exegesis of the possession episodes, but by recurring once more to a New Testament pattern of thought and speech.

The student of the New Testament soon learns of the prominence of the theme of the Reign of God which Jesus proclaimed, and of the identification of the coming of the Reign with the coming of Jesus which the disciples made. To the Reign of God is opposed another Reign or Kingdom which the Reign of God attacks and gradually vanquishes. World history becomes a history of the conflict of these two Reigns, the Reign of God and the Reign of Satan, the conflict which Ignatius of Loyola dramatized in his meditation on Two Standards. The ultimate and total victory of the Reign of God occurs in the eschatological end of days.

The Reign of Satan is the reign of evil in the broadest sense;

Satan is the agent of all that mankind calls evil. This includes not only the moral evil of sin but the whole package of human suffering. In Romans 6-7 Paul calls it the Reign of Sin and Death, and the coupling of the two should be noticed. Were there no sin, there would be no death. It is not enough for the Reign of God—the saving act of God in Christ Jesus—to overcome sin; God must also overcome death. In I Corinthians 15:26 Paul calls Death the last adversary to be overcome, after Christ has destroyed every Rule and Authority and Power. These words refer to elements of the Reign of Satan; that Gregory the Great included them among his nine choirs of angels suggests that Gregory sometimes read his Bible too rapidly.

Death is, as Job called him, the king of terrors, and he is accompanied by a retinue of afflicting agents of disease and corruption. This is the area over which Satan reigns unchecked until the coming of Christ; it is indeed a vast and systematized expansion of the ancient belief in demonic power to do harm to man. Against this mighty host only the Reign of God can move. Hence Jesus moves not only against sin but against disease. In an early episode in Mark (2:1-12) Jesus greets the paralytic with the announcement that his sins are forgiven. This is treated as a blasphemous claim to the power of God. Jesus demonstrates his power to forgive sins by curing the paralytic. The paralytic is under the power of the Reign of Satan in soul and body.

Jesus asserts his power to turn back the Reign of Satan by attacking him on both fronts, the Reign of Sin and the Reign of Death. Whenever human misery is removed or lightened, Satan's Reign suffers a defeat, a token of the eschatological defeat which is promised. In this thought pattern not only every cure of disease but every work of mercy, every feeding of the hungry and clothing of the naked and sheltering of the homeless is a rollback of the Reign of Satan, an exorcism of the demon.

Yet I must say that this is a mythological pattern, and I hasten to say that I do not mean it is false. It is an attempt to present reality in the image of events which are rather enduring realities symbolized by the events. The reality is the evil in the world, which is so vast and so often seems to render man helpless that man is moved to attribute it to cosmic forces greater than himself. In this imagery there is the danger of dualism, a danger which the New Testament does not entirely remove. In much of Christian belief Satan has become an anti-God. If he is real, that is what he must be; if he is a symbol, he is not. The evil in the world is not the product of a cosmic personal principle of evil. It is the work of the only cosmic evildoer, man himself.

The myth of Satan has its value, but not when Satan is made a scapegoat for what man does. We really do not believe we are so bad that Satan and his demons are mythological symbols of ourselves. I have said half-seriously that if Satan ever spent some time in human company he would flee back to hell in terror as a safer place. It was half-serious. I have lived long enough to know that I need no help from a demonic tempter to prompt me to do evil. What I do not think of myself will be suggested to me by my fellow men. If we want to have an encounter with a live and active devil, we have only to look in the mirror. There is the enemy of God. Christopher Morley once had one of his characters say, "And to think Christ died for the likes of you."

I do not expect this interpretation to be cordially received; and this helps to explain what would have happened to Jesus if, instead of accepting the common patterns of thought and speech, he had said: "Do not let the devils worry you. You are the only devils there are, and that is something to worry about." We should now be mature enough to recognize the reality behind the mythological symbol. The challenge to the Reign of God may thus appear as much greater than we thought.

As a footnote the book of the Revelation of John should be briefly noted. This book, which could be illustrated only by an artist like Breughel, seems to have employed every resource of demonology known to the author; and they were many. The nightmare visions of the writer attempted to portray the horrors of the Reign of Satan so that no further portrayal would ever be needed. The angelic army is necessary in his mythology to overcome the demonic hosts. One advantage of the book is that the symbolism is so exaggerated that the mythology becomes evident.

Yet is it so exaggerated? Would the writer of the Revelations, or artists like Breughel, Dürer and Doré have been able to respond to the newspaper photographs and television views of multiple deaths in automobile accidents, or grinning idiots with guns standing over dead bodies in Beirut or Israel, or older photographs of Dresden or Belsen or Hiroshima, or pedestrians stepping over the corpses of the starved in India? No, perhaps the Revelation of John did not color the mythology of evil too deeply. It does leave one wondering what Satan could do for us. If this be rationalism, make the most of it. I am sick of excuses for the wicked things we do.

_____  _____

# ANCESTORS AND ANCESTOR WORSHIP

**W**HEN I first visited the southern states, a friend in the South told me that ancestor worship was the established religion in Mobile and Charleston. I hope any readers who might dwell in these two cities will be amused rather than angered by this recounting of what is very probably an old joke, and one that is somewhat unfair. In these cities, at least, they do not have to search out the ancestors to worship. I read that genealogical research is a very active and profitable industry. European tours always include some Americans who are making the trip in search of a family home or a family tree. They seem oblivious of the risk of discovering that great-grandfather rode with Quantrill or was lynched as a horsethief.

These observations, neither profound nor based upon extensive research, set the ground for my remarks on genealogical research in the Bible. Genealogical research was an active industry in the composition of the Old Testament; and even Jesus was endowed with a genealogy which made him a descendant of David—indeed, with two genealogies. We may treat these as a midrash on the messianic title "Son of David."

The believer who embarks on the task of reading the whole Bible is early dismayed by the genealogies as well as by the building of the tabernacle (twice!) and by the ritual laws of Leviticus. It is only fair to the ancient scribes to ask what purpose the genealogical lists were thought to serve. The most obvious purpose was to fill gaps. The books of the Old

Testament contain an uninterrupted list of names from Adam to the twelve sons of Jacob. Some of the scribes may have intended to carry the list uninterrupted to the high priests in the Second Temple, but it is not clear that this is what they meant. When one composes artificial genealogies, there is really no limit on one's ambitions. When one has nothing but names, one is not totally without information; and when the names are given without any order, one may arrange them in that order which seems best.

A second purpose, surely, the biblical genealogies share with the modern American search for one's roots in the past. This is to some degree a search for identity, clan or tribal identity rather than personal identity; it is also a search for authenticity in a way which I find hard to describe. We hope to show that we and ours have established those rights and perquisites which are deemed proper to long-term residents. A third and more practical purpose is to establish claims to property and other rights more intangible. I doubt that the average American who turns the genealogists loose on his family tree really expects them to come up with a patent of nobility, although there is an obvious pleasure if they do.

A fourth purpose is seen in a passage found twice in the Old Testament (Ezra 2:59-63 and Nehemiah 7:61-65). Here we read of some claimants to the priestly office that they could not prove their Israelite descent from the genealogies. The genealogies were certainly available, and there must have been other claims which were settled by appeal to the documents. The modern student of the Bible wonders who prepared these records and from what materials, and where and in whose custody they were preserved. If one assumes that the interminable genealogies of I Chronicles 1-9 represent such records, then they were largely artificial.

In the list of the choir called the sons of Heman in I Chronicles one section of names is a line of a hymn, turned into personal names (I Chronicles 25:4). Yet these names are seriously given sons and brothers (each to the number of twelve) later in the same chapter. If these were the genealogies used to prove one's lineage, one wonders how anyone failed to qualify. Even if they were more dependable than the genealogies of the chronicler, one has to wonder where the records which made it possible to compile them were kept and how they were preserved during the somewhat unsettled years which preceded Nehemiah and Ezra.

Against this background it is not difficult to understand the interest in ancestors manifested in the book of Genesis. For various reasons, some of which I hope will become clear in the following pages, this interest suggests a later rather than an earlier date for the rise of ancestor or heroic tales. To appeal again to our contemporary fellow Americans, it may be a safe generalization to say that the American does not begin to wonder who his ancestors were until he thinks he has succeeded well enough in life to risk comparison with his forebears. We shall see that the stories of the patriarchs must come from a people who dwelt in Canaan, and that the lack of information about the patriarchs suggests that they are remote in time from the stories about them.

The ancestral heroes are four in number: Abraham, Isaac, Jacob and Joseph. They are connected in a chain of lineal descent; and we may as well say at once that no biblical scholar, whatever he may think of the historical quality of the patriarchal stories, believes that the lineal connection between the four patriarchs is historical. They do not even have the same ethnic background; as far as we can see, Abraham was an Amorite and Jacob an Aramean; and while Joseph has been given a Hebrew name and a Hebrew genealogy, in other respects he appears as an Egyptian. He also through his own sons occupies two places in the fellowship of Jacob's twelve sons. The time involved is loosely dealt with, and the patriarchs are credited with ages which exceed the bounds of credibility. The geography is good but vague as long as it deals with Canaan.

Through the patriarchs the Israelites recognize their kinship with neighboring peoples: Edom (Esau), Moab and Ammon (Lot, kinsman of Abraham). Their closest kin, the Canaanites, are not recognized, and the undisguised venomous hatred of the Canaanites throughout most of the Old Testament creates problems which have not yet been solved. Very probably George Mendenhall is right in seeing in this a reflection of the hatred of peasant serfs against a landowning aristocracy. It is a problem for this opinion that the ancestral stories do not furnish the historical background for such a situation.

Hardly any scholar doubts that the artificial lineal genealogy of the patriarchs was a tacit recognition of the somewhat mixed antecedents of the people of Israel, a recognition which contradicts any ideal of purity of blood. When John the Baptist is said to tell the Jews that God could raise up sons of Abraham from these stones, he perhaps had a better foundation for poking fun at Jewish pride of ancestry than he knew. Ezekiel (16:3) said to Jerusalem that its origins were Canaanite, its father Amorite and its mother Hittite, thus affirming the despised Canaanite ancestry as well as other "Gentiles" in the mixed bag of Israel's forebears. The gibe suggests that pride of ancestry was there to be mocked even in the early sixth century. No doubt it was; a law of Deuteronomy 23:3-6 prohibits admission to "the assembly of the Lord" for a number of named foreign peoples—some until a defined period of residence in Israel has elapsed and some permanently. This exclusion is based upon some biblical traditions of relations between these peoples and their ancestors. It is interesting that these include just those peoples with whom the Israelites had a kinship relation, and that the traditions upon which the exclusion was based are of doubtful historical value. Ancient enmities have sometimes been sustained long after the real reasons were forgotten, and new reason had to be invented.

It is tempting to say that a people is known by the heroes it venerates. I resist the temptation because the gallery of heroes shows a tedious recurrence of fighting men like the dull-witted, muscular, perpetual adolescent Achilles of the Iliad. Perhaps this tells us something about mankind rather than about particular peoples. Actually, the "wily" Odysseus was more the ideal Greek hero than Achilles. But every Heroic Age shows a distressing similarity to the other Heroic ages. When Cervantes did in the heroes of chivalry, Spain was well embarked on a new heroic age whose heroes were in no way chivalrous, and well equipped to deal with the new English heroes who were pirates.

I dwell on this recurring theme of the hero who was really a bushwacker and a cutthroat because the Israelite patriarchs do not fit into this gallery of heroes. The hero does appear in Israelite folklore. The heroes of the conquest and the book of Judges were killers worthy of inclusion in the gallery; Saul and David began their careers as bandit cheiftains who became great as mercenary warriors. But the ancestors who were venerated are represented as men of peace. The only story of prowess at arms is the defeat of five invading kings by Abraham and his 318 retainers in Genesis 14. The story bristles with historical problems which scholars have not yet solved to general satisfaction, and one of the problems is that it is out of character with the other Abraham stories. If Abraham could muster 318 armed men, he was a bandit chieftain of the stature of Gideon or Saul or David. Yet elsewhere he appears as a prosperous herdsman, neither giving nor taking offense, unable to protect his wife from being kidnapped.

This particular story was a favorite, for it was told twice of Abraham and once of Isaac. It is scarcely to be compared with the rape of Helen, the most willing victim of rape in all history and literature, the face which launched a thousand ships and burnt the topless towers of Ilium. But the theme is the same, the theme that our girls are so beautiful they are desired by all men. In any case, Abraham does not launch a thousand ships or even assemble his 318 thugs; he plans on his wife making him agreeable to the potentate who kidnapped her.

The other allusion to feats of arms is found in the last words of Jacob in Genesis 48:22, it refers to a conquest of land from the Amorites. There is no allusion to this incident elsewhere in the stories of Jacob. Jacob's brother Esau achieved armed strength much earlier; when Jacob heard that Esau was coming to meet him with 400 men, he divided his caravan hoping to save one third at least; this is hardly the hero who conquered the Amorities with his sword and his bow. This suggests that there may have been more tradition of arms and battle than Genesis has preserved.

As we shall see, all the traditions of conquest were put together in one series. This allows the patriarchs to appear not only as men of peace but as men of God, to whom God speaks and whom God protects. This is dominant in the stories about Abraham. It is less prominent in the stories about Jacob, who is a more complex character than Abraham. Isaac in any case is a difficult figure to analyze. He is hardly more than a shadow, and everything which happens to him is found in the adventures of Abraham or of Jacob. What importance he has is the same importance which Abraham and Jacob have; their importance is religious. They are mediators of revelation.

The revelation is mediated only to their family, family here meaning the larger kinship group of clan and tribe. By an artificial calculation the household of Jacob at its entrance into Egypt is reckoned at seventy. The revelation is addressed to no others because it does not concern others. It is a promise to Abraham, Isaac and Jacob of the blessing of God which will be realized in the possession of a land in which the patriarchs are foreign residents and in the growth of their family into a great people. We shall have occasion elsewhere in this series to consider the place of the promise in Israelite and biblical belief. But when one tries to sum up the content of the "revelation" to the patriarchs, it is the promise. According to at least one Israelite tradition the patriarchs did not know the name of the God who spoke to them, the name by which he was addressed in Israel. He was the God of Abraham and Isaac and Jacob, interested in other people only when they came in touch with those whom he had chosen.

Within this framework Abraham becomes a heroic figure because he believed the promise; Abraham remains throughout the Bible the hero of faith which Genesis portrays him as being. Neither wandering nor famine nor childlessness nor weakness in the face of power is able to shake his faith. The great test of his faith was the command to sacrifice his son Isaac, a story told with unusual skill and dramatic tension.

From what we have said about the probable relations and historical quality of Abraham and Isaac, it is evident that we do not think we are discussing a historical incident; and scholars are not agreed on what appear to be several layers of meaning successively imposed upon the story. The last level, apparent to the Bible reader, makes Abraham a hero of faith.

This is not the heroic mold in which Jacob is cast. Like Odysseus, Jacob is the wily and the crafty man who obtains his ends by his wits rather than by his strength. The story does not mean to deny him heroic strength; he meets Rachel for the first time when he removes a stone from the mouth of a well which can be removed only by the combined efforts of a number of shepherds. The story of the duel of wits between two unscrupulous men, Laban and Jacob, which the hero finally wins, must have been a delight to the Israelites; if it was, it tells us something about them. This does not imply that admiration for the overreacher was peculiarly Israelite; all folklores have heroes like Rumpelstiltskin. Samson, the muscleman preeminent in Israelite folklore, is praised more for outwitting the Philistines than for outpushing them, a form of slave humor which is found wherever there is slavery. Possibly the prophet Hosea (Hosea 12:2-4) later had doubts about some of Jacob's feats of wit. His name was explained by a surely imaginative etymology as "the Tripper," hardly a flattering title, and connected with the episode of his birth. He is, as we remarked, hardly a hero of faith.

The adventure of Jacob at the crossing of the River Jabbok (Genesis 32:22-32) presents problems peculiar to itself. The being with whom Jacob wrestles is not called an angel of God; Jewish and Christian piety have refused to recognize what is probably a demon which guards the frontier. Jacob is crossing the line which later becomes the frontier of Israel.

When he crosses it he acquires the name of Israel; and he is opposed at the crossing. It has been suggested that a foreign myth has been applied to Jacob here.

Jacob is the father of twelve sons, the eponymous ancestor of the twelve tribes of Israel. There is no dispute that this is an artificial genealogy. We have noticed that the two sons of Joseph replace him in the list of twelve, forcing the exclusion of Levi in one reckoning, of Simeon in another. The questions which these two tribes raise cannot be treated at sufficient length within the limits of this essay. I suggest that anyone who wonders about this ambiguity of the twelve tribes write down at once the names of the thirteen colonies which seceded from the British Crown in 1776. Most people cannot, and very probably most Israelites could not name the twelve tribes. Judah appears in Genesis 37 as an independent landowner of some substance, not one of twelve sons living under the dominion of their father.

Joseph furnishes the necessary link between Israel and Egypt. If Israel came out of Egypt, it must have got in there somehow. The story is the proverbial story of the rich uncle who materializes to save his family in critical need. It is so much a story according to type that historians have trouble taking it as historical. Such stories are found in ancient Egyptian litera; the Egyptians had a taste for such moralizing romances, and it is not impossible that the story was borrowed from an Egyptian source. If it was, the Israelite failed, no doubt from lack of understanding, to preserve much of the authentic Egyptian coloring which we find in Egyptian literature. The story of Joseph in its present form was told by a non-Egyptian. But it does get the sons of Jacob (or the sons of Israel) into Egypt, where they must be in order to have an exodus.

I called the story of Joseph a moralizing romance, and it perhaps should be pointed out what the moral thrust of the story is. The virtue of Joseph is that peculiar biblical virtue now translated as "covenant love," in the older versions "loving-kindness." This version fails to render the element of kinship or covenant association on which the attitude is based. Coupled with the noun "fidelity," as it often is, it is the virtue of steady and dependable loyalty which one expects from a kinsman or a covenant partner. It does not mean love, which in Hebrew designates rather the passionate feeling of love; loving-kindness is operative and proved love. The ideal loving-kindness endures through the treatment which Joseph endured from his brothers, and forgives them for the sake of the common father. For our tastes it seems that the young Joseph is presented as an intolerably vain and spoiled child; but for the ancient scribe it was simply a precocious exhibition of that insight which enabled him to rise to the position of vizier in Egypt.

I said that Joseph appears as an Egyptian; religion is never a problem for him. This among other things makes one wonder whether the successful lost brother was not in the earliest form of the story an Egyptian magnate who granted the clan from Canaan permission to live on the fringes of Egyptian territory. One need know little about rural life to know how the Egyptians felt about sheep and goats pasturing in the acres which they cultivated with so much skill and toil. I realize that this takes away any base in fact for the moralizing romance about loving kindness, a virtue quite necessary in a kinship group; but such questions were not asked in the circles in which the story arose. This is not meant to be an effort to reconstruct the presence of the sons of Jacob in Egypt by rationalization, but simply a guess at some authentic memory which may be buried under layers of retelling.

The reader may ask at this point how much genuine history is left of the patriarchs. It has been my purpose to point out that there is not much. Yet scholars do not treat the material merely as literary invention; and I realize that the adverb "merely" can be applied to Oedipus or Hamlet or David Copperfield. They too are "merely" literary invention. Yet historians used to think that the story of the Iliad was a story "once upon a time in a country far away." Now they know there was a Troy, and that there were wars about it; Helen, unfortunately, remains fictitious. Homer wrote long after this war—if indeed he wrote—but the historian sifts through his material, one might almost say, for what he tells us without intending to.

The names of the patriarchs are real, most probably; their geography is not the geography of imagination. There were stories told about them; and quite probably there were stories told about them which were first told about someone else. Their religion, the object of major interest, is not merely a retrojection of later Israelite belief and practice; the scribes made an effort, not too successful, to reconstruct the religion of their ancestors. They did remove everything which they themselves found offensive; the ancestors show none of the mythological polytheism of the ancient Near East. They are described not only as ancestors but as precursors, foreshadowing in some ways the religious and the social experiences of their descendants.

The narratives are meant to be edifying, although they may not always succeed for us. But the motif of faith, which I mentioned for Abraham, does dominate the religious picture. If one believes that God can and will do what he promises to do, then one can expect to be treated by God with that consideration anyone gives to another who believes his word. The scribes did not yet have the word commitment; but we may use it, in spite of its abuse. When he wrote that Abraham went at God's word, a God he did not know, out of his country and his kindred to the land which God would show him, he described a commitment. In the religion of the scribe people felt that a God who would knock flat on his back a man who would do that was hardly deserving of further interest.

# 7

# THIS LAND IS MINE

OVER ten years ago the words by which this chapter is entitled were the key line of the theme song of the motion picture *Exodus*, based on the novel of the same title. One saw scenes of shiploads of Jewish emigrants from Europe; the song presumably articulated their thoughts. The authors and producers intended to evoke the biblical exodus from Egypt, omitting the unimportant detail that the ancestors of those who said this land was theirs had not resided in that land for one to two thousand years. It is now impossible to discuss the biblical narratives of the exodus and conquest without adverting to the contemporary reenactment of these narratives; for that is what the contemporary scene is, and that is what it is intended to be.

There is in the Near East and has been for centuries a clear social and cultural division, expressed in two Arabic words which we translate as the "Desert" and the "Sown." The Desert in this phrase does not mean the rocky, sandy wastes of the central Arabian peninsula where nobody lives; it means the steppes, the semi-arid plateaus adjacent to settled areas, covered part of the year by seasonal grass. The two words designate not only two geographical areas but two ways of life, two cultures.

The culture of the Desert is the culture of the Bedu; the culture of the Sown is the culture of the Fellahin. The Bedu are nomadic herdsmen who live off their flocks of sheep and herds of goats. They follow the seasonal grass and where this fails, they settle around the grass and water of isolated oases.

They do not build houses but live in tents made of animal skins, which they call houses of hair. The Fellahin are peasants, tenant farmers. They live in villages and cultivate the soil, never farther away than walking distance from their houses. The relations between the two cultures are amicable and hostile at once; they have lived as neighbors for some thousands of years, and the hostility does not run deep.

Students of Near Eastern history and culture warn us not to transfer thoughtlessly modern social conditions to the ancient Near East. They point out that the domestication of the camel, comparatively modern in the ancient Near East, was nearly as revolutionary in the culture of the Bedu as the introduction of the motorcar was in Europe and North America. With reservations made, one can still see nomadic herdsmen (meaning keepers of sheep and goats) in the modern Near East, and one can recognize many features of their life which are alluded to in the Bible. There was an ancient version of the Desert and the Sown; and the basic difference was the ownership and cultivation of land.

The earliest traditions of Israelite origins derived Israel not from the Sown but from the Desert. Questions may now be asked and have been asked about the historical validity of these traditions; but there is no doubt that Abraham, Isaac and Jacob appear as nomadic herdsmen, and that Jacob and his "sons" were admitted into Egypt as nomadic herdsmen, not as peasants; this is the unambiguous meaning of Genesis 47:1-6. It was not without a certain interest that I once heard an Israeli tour guide describe Israeli plans to make the survival of the culture of the modern Bedu, who represent the way of life of the patriarchs, impossible. I was interested because the nomadic herdsman has buried every conqueror of Canaan.

There is a connection between land and identity. Old

Testament persons are introduced by giving the name of their father; Greeks of the classical period were introduced by the name of their city. The modern man or woman is often asked where he or she is from; often, when I answer Chicago, I am told, "No, I mean where are you really from." Before World War I the French used to speak of the rape of Alsace-Lorraine, which is pushing the metaphor rather hard. The partition of Poland was remembered and healed, not to universal satisfaction, after nearly one hundred and fifty years. It is not so surprising that blood is now shed over the much more recent partition of Ireland. The Scot is not English and the Sicilian is not Italian. I hesitate from sheer terror to illustrate ethnic and geographic identity from the lands of eastern Europe. It does seem that in a civilized culture the question of identity is answered by answering the question where you are from. In a tribal culture it is answered by identifying your relatives.

This observation, which may pass for digression, is intended to suggest that when Israelite literature implies a connection of identity between the people of Israel and, in turn, between the people of God and the land of God, it is entirely foreign to ways of thought known to other peoples. The legend of "The Wandering Jew," which became a book title, does have an implication which is strange to these ways of thought. Why not a legend of the wandering Irish, or the wandering Pole, or the wandering Spaniard? Simply because the Irish and the Poles and the Spanish have made homes for themselves outside of "their" lands; the Jew, once he is exiled from the land of Israel, can be at home nowhere. I am not attempting to affirm this implication, but simply to point out that it is there, and that it has biblical roots.

In a previous discussion of the patriarchs I did not dwell

upon their association with the land, since it is too important to be treated briefly. The land of Canaan, which has also gone by the names of Israel and Palestine, is traditionally the Promised Land. When Abraham was first called by God, the call was to leave his land and kinship and go to a land which God would show him. When he arrived at Shechem in Canaan, God identified this as the land which he would give Abraham's descendants. The promise is repeated several times in the story of Abraham, due mostly to the fact that the promise appears in all the literary sources from which the book of Genesis was compiled. The promise is combined with the promise of a posterity numerous enough to possess the land. The promises are repeated to Isaac and Jacob, again in the several literary sources of The Pentateuch, with so little variation in wording that one recognizes the presence of conventional formulae.

The patriarchs covered a good part of Canaan in their "wanderings," the journeys with their flocks from one pasture to another; but they did not cover the entire land of Israel. Abraham is found south of Shechem, centrally located in Canaan. The places associated with him lie entirely in what became the territory of Judah and south of it, mostly in the semi-arid steppes to the south called the Negeb. In the future Judah he is associated with Mamre near Hebron, a city which the tradition recognized as not yet founded at this early period.

Isaac is associated entirely with the Negeb; he does not appear north of Beersheba, the traditional southern boundary of the Land of Israel. Jacob is found farther to the north, he is associated with Shechem and Dothan, and we have referred in a previous essay to his entrance into the future land of Israel from the east. The identification of Ephrath, where Rachel was buried, with Bethlehem in Genesis 35:19 is now recognized as a gloss; Eprath is to be located in the territory which bore the name of the son of Rachel, Benjamin. This certainly leaves much of Israel without any patriarchal association, and it does not remove the ambiguities of the boundaries of the Promised Land. As we shall see, these boundaries were ultimately defined in broader terms than the stories of the patriarchs would suggest.

I draw attention again to the fact that the patriarchs appear as nomadic herdsmen, not as dwellers in towns or landowners. In Genesis 23 the purchase of land for a burying ground by Abraham is narrated with great circumstance and solemnity; it is a valuable little picture of bargaining in the ancient Near East. The importance of the story is that it relates the first acquisition of landed property by an ancestor of Israel; and it is not unimportant that it is represented as purchased with all legal solemnity. No similar transaction is related about Isaac and Jacob. The episode is found in the latest of the literary sources of Genesis, called the Priestly source. This does not mean that the late source could not have preserved an earlier story.

It is a little difficult to explain this insistence on the legal purchase of a piece of landed property in a territory which God promised to Abraham's descendants, except that the urgency was there. No similar urgency was felt by the scribe who reported the burial of Rachel by Jacob in land which was not his own. We noticed in an earlier chapter that Jacob is once credited with acquisition of land from the Amorites by conquest (Genesis 48:22), the title to land which is both the most secure and the least legal. We noticed also that this has no echo elsewhere in the narratives.

In the story of the exodus Moses leads the people out of

Egypt into the land promised to their fathers. The traditions have not preserved perfect consistency in this connection, and it is unnecessary to go into details concerning this problem; the whole theory of the exodus and settlement depends on the assumption that a group of emigrants from Egypt moved into territory which God has promised to their ancestors and had now ordered them to possess. That the actual course of events was more complex we are sure, but we are unable to reconstruct the actual course of events. The late Martin Noth traced five different and originally independent themes in the Pentateuch: liberation from Egypt, entrance into Canaan, promise to the fathers, bringing through the desert, and revelation at Sinai. These have been combined in a way which makes it impossible even to trace their original presentation, much less to reconstruct the events which lie behind them. We are now dealing with only two of these themes, and we observe how they are connected with liberation from Egypt.

The theology of the land receives its clearest definition in the book of Deuteronomy. Critics think this book was written in consciousness of the possible loss of the land threatened by major political powers of the eighth and seventh centuries, a threat which was fully realized in the sixth century. Deuteronomy represents the land as the sheer gift of God to Israel, requiring no military or diplomatic effort on the part of Israel. God makes resistance impossible by sending a panic upon the land's inhabitants, and Israel has only to take possession from a helpless population. But both the possession and the retention of the Promised Land are restrained by conditions explicitly proposed by Deuteronomy. The conditions are fidelity to the law of God as stated in Deuteronomy 12-26, the terms of the covenant. If the Israelites are unfaith-

ful to the covenant, they become subject to the curses recited
with satisfactory fullness in Deuteronomy 28:15-68; 29:2-29;
31:16-29. The ultimate curse is expulsion from the land
which has been given them.

Certainly to ignore this theme in speaking of promise and
fulfillment is to distort it. The promise is explicitly conditioned,
and it is revoked if the conditions are violated. The work
called the Deuteronomic history, by which is meant the historical books from Joshua to 2 Kings (with Deuteronomy as a
prologue) was written, as the same Martin Noth explained it,
to show that the story of the judgment which fell upon Israel
and Judah and removed them from their land was a judgment delivered upon an entirely deserving people. In the
words of another Israelite poet, the author of Job, the Lord
gave, the Lord took away; blessed be the name of the Lord.

The biblical account of the actual possession of the land is
an account of a conquest. Many modern scholars regard this
as the earliest effort to reconstruct the history of the origins of
the people of Israel in the land of Israel. There are many
elements in the reconstruction which are unsatisfactory. Part
of the story reflects the theory of the land as the gift of God;
thus God divides the Jordan as he divided the Red Sea, and
walls of Jericho collapse at the sound of the horns. In other
episodes a more or less real battle is described. The geography of the stories does not permit us to call it a conquest of
Canaan, although some realism appears in the recognition
that the earliest possession did not extend to the ideal boundaries of the Promised Land.

But the "conquest" as narrated does not allow the entirely
unreal description of the tribal allotments made by Joshua,
which describe the survey and division of land which has
been completely emptied by its population. The allotment,

however, does take place within the historic boundaries of the land of Israel, as far as we can determine them. Deuteronomy excludes the kingdoms of Edom, Moab and Ammon because God did not include them in the donation. The disturbing presence of the Philistines was not dealt with so neatly. The boundaries of Israel according to Deuteronomy do not include the conquests of David, which the scribes recognized as conquests lost under David's successors. Again one perceives a certain realism in Deuteronomy's theology of the gift of the land.

A brief note on later Israelite presence in the land should be added. The land lost to Israel by the conquests of Assyria and Babylon was never recovered. A small Jewish settlement established under Persian government was limited to the neighborhood of Jerusalem. The valid claim of the Samaritans to be of Israelite descent was never recognized by the Jews. The only independent Jewish government, again over only part of Israel, appeared in the Maccabean revolt of the second century, and this government was as independent as the great powers allowed it to be. The land became Roman in 63 B.C. Except for two brief Jewish rebellions in 66-70 and 132-135 A.D., the land was never again Jewish until a Jewish state was established in 1948 by violence, like all its predecessors.

The late Gerhard von Rad published some years ago a monograph on the theological theme called the holy war. The expression ought to shock us but does not. The theme is nowhere summarized in the Old Testament. Von Rad found that its elements were a war of all Israel (not just some of the tribes) summoned by religious leadership, consecration of the warriors and the imposition of a condition of holiness, including abstinence from alcoholic beverages, the barber and from sex, the consecration of booty to God and the killing of all living beings. Strange as it may seem, the last elements were an attempt to raise the ethical level of ancient war, which was candidly robbery. So is ours, but it is less candid. I would add that the holy war was fought only to acquire or to defend the Promised Land. This is not supported by the only holy war found outside of Joshua and Judges, the war of Saul against the Amalekites in I Samuel 15. But if I am right in adding this element, then the holy war is closely associated with the topic of our discussion, the acquisition and possession of the land. (See also chapter 19.)

The wars attributed to Joshua are holy wars, including the element of sure and nearly effortless victory. In the holy war God is an invincible warrior. As we noticed, he sends a panic which renders the enemy helpless. Also it is the holy war by which Israel takes possession of the gift. Joshua can allot the land because there is nobody there. The Hebrew word which we translate "ban" means the extinction of all life and the dedication of booty to God—that is to the sanctuary. The Israelites were repulsed in their first attack on Ai because an Israelite kept a portion of the booty. Otherwise the Israelites had no problems; if Joshua needed overtime at the battle of Gibeon (Joshua 10), God made the sun stand still. In the battle of Deborah and Barak (Judges 4-5), possibly another instance of a holy war, God fights for Israel by sending an unexpected rainfall which mires the chariots of the Canaanites. I observed that the holy war is not invoked in the conquests of David, although the abstinence of Uriah (2 Sam. 11) suggests that some archaic practices were retained after they had lost meaning. The wars with the Philistines had every reason to be declared holy wars, and it seems they were not. The reason may be that the Israelites were generally unable to handle the Philistines.

One asks how real and how historical this savage theology of the holy war may have been. The ancient world knew the atrocities of war, although frankly the more one studies them the more one doubts that the ancient world knew them as well as we do. The ancient war I have called a plundering expedition; and since slaves were the most valuable form of plunder, in most wars thoughtless killing would have been regarded as imprudent. The Assyrians are themselves the principal witnesses for their legendary atrocities; and some historians think they made themselves out to be worse than they were to frighten both their friends and their enemies. In fact there is no report of an Assyrian treatment of a defeated city which matches the atrocities described at Jericho and Ai and Hazor. This leaves one with the feeling that the Israelites were worse than the Assyrians from a higher religious motive; and it is things like this which make people wonder about religion.

The Bible reader may in this respect be comforted by the general agreement of biblical historians that the atrocities of Jericho and Ai and Hazor are unhistorical. This still leaves the theology of the holy war as a moral ideal. And it should be observed that all readers of the Old Testament have found room for the holy war in their moral theology. The Christians of the ages of faith (an unfortunate phrase) offered Moslems and Jews the alternatives of baptism or execution, and launched Crusades with the clear purpose of exterminating the unbeliever. The Moslems launched their holy wars against the unbelievers. The biblical theologian finds traces of the theology of the holy war in modern Israeli foreign policy. In the western world there is a tendency to turn every war into a crusade, even if the war is about as moral as the gangster wars of Chicago of the 1920s. Because Hitler was so beastly the bombing of Dresden became a crusade. Because the lives

of American boys are so sacred we could exact the lives of
Japanese men, women and infant children as their ransom.

The United States fought its holy war against native Americans. Extinction was intended but not achieved. That I forget
the name of the historian does not prevent me from stealing
his remark that the Europeans went after the native Americans exactly as they went after the fauna. I have seen both
Sherman and Sheridan quoted as saying that the only good
Indian is a dead Indian. There is no doubt that the saying
expressed their thoughts. But they were no more than faithful
instruments of a national policy which truly expressed the will
of the people. Whatever Leiutenant Calley did at My Lai—
and the laws of libel allow me to say that he did something—
he did as the heir of a military tradition which includes Col-
onel John Chivington and Brevet Major General George
Armstrong Custer.

It is because I believe Jesus did not deliver a new law that I
can say it is wrong to think that we ought to treat the Law as
terminal. The principles of life which we attribute to Jesus
make the theology of the holy war quite impossible. The life
which Jesus proclaimed cannot be fostered, advanced or
protected by any kind of war, holy or unholy. Jesus taught
men how to die, not how to kill. The holy war has certainly
been a major block in proclamation of authentic and integral
Christianity. "God wills it" was the war cry of the First
Crusade. Should it have been clear in the eleventh century
that he did not will it? They had the same evidence about the
will of God that we have. They had the same obstacles to
seeing and accepting it that we have. Our success in breaking
down those obstacles is not such that it permits me to pa-
tronize the men of the eleventh century as not very well
advanced Christians.

# THE MANY FACES OF MOSES

$T$OURISTS who take the trouble to find the church of San Pietro in Vincoli of Rome, which is not easily accessible either from the Vatican or from the Via Vittorio Veneto, generally do it because they want to see the Moses of Michaelangelo. They are often disappointed that the statue is not of the heroic size which they expect. I fear that some readers will think that I am trying to reduce the heroic size of Moses, and I may as well reduce at once one of the heroic features of the statue. The horns of Moses (one of his many faces) come from an ancient misunderstanding of a Hebrew word which means that the face of Moses was glowing or shining, not that he sprouted horns.

The horns are not the only distortion which has defaced Moses over the last two or three thousand years; and it is my intention to deal here with the major distortions. Moses in the Bible can be said to appear in four roles: as author, as liberator, as mediator of covenant and revelation, and as lawgiver. I mention the role of author first because it is the easiest to dismiss. Moses had been accepted as author of the first five books of the Bible—known as the five books of Moses or the Pentateuch—since late pre-Christian Judaism. In the early 1900s the Pontifical Biblical Commission forbade Catholic teachers and writers to propose anything else. Since that time scholars universally—and that includes Catholics—reject Moses as the author of these or any other books. We cannot be sure that we have one written word which can be attributed to Moses. If scholarly consensus means anything, it should certainly be meaningful here.

The denial of Moses as an author has certain consequences. We cannot think of the stories of Moses as autobiog-
raphical. We cannot even think of them as contemporary with
the events; again we deal with a consensus of scholars. The
task of locating the elements of the books of Moses in place
and time is too complex to be treated here; for there is
scholarly disagreement.

One may ask, if Moses did not write the Pentateuch, who
did; and it is not just a smart answer to say that no one did. In
the five books we can trace four major literary strands. Each
of these has been compiled both from pre-existing writings
and from some oral traditions, from cultic literature and from
songs and from collections of law. These materials were not
assembled into their present form until the fifth century B.C.
The authors were anonymous, as all ancient scribes were.
The whole process is thought to have taken about four
hundred years. In this sense I mean the Pentateuch had no
author.

We turn, then, to the role of Moses as liberator, the man
who led a people (not yet surely known by the name Israel)
out of bondage in Egypt into the Promised Land of Canaan.
The story has been given a specious realism by the production genius of the late Cecil B. DeMille; and moviegoers have
rarely doubted that God can do what DeMille could do. The
producer's genius glossed over some of the difficulties with
which the story bristles. Nothing that we know of the ancient
Egyptians suggests that they were capable of genocide; they
were too humane for that, and besides it was economically
insane.

Moses probably had an Egyptian name and he was reared
as an Egyptian. The story of his birth and family (which has a
remarkable resemblance to the legend of Sargon of Akkad)

gives him a Hebrew ancestry. The "slavery" from which he liberates his countrymen was the ordinary life of the Egyptian peasant, who seems to have been more contented with his lot than most peasants. The story of the plagues is loaded with improbabilities, of which the greatest is that a man who disposed of such resources should have that much trouble with the king of Egypt (whose name is unknown to the author). The death of the first-born, we think, could not have occurred without leaving some trace in other records than Exodus 12.

More troublesome than the improbabilities is the fact that the authors of the plague stories betray a rather comprehensive ignorance of Egypt. No one walked in and out of the presence of the king of Egypt as Moses and Aaron are said to do; the king of Egypt was a god, and one of his officers had what we would call the function of appointments secretary. The Nile has exhibited a regular pattern of behavior since the dawn of recorded history, only now likely to be altered by the colossal folly of the high dam at Aswan. When we do not recognize the behavior described in the first plague, we think it is because the author described something which neither he nor anyone else had ever seen. Efforts to rationalize the crossing of the sea have not been convincing; and Bible readers are not impressed if they are told that Moses led the Hebrews through a marsh.

The "wanderings" in the desert of Sinai are scarcely credible. No one would pass through Sinai to get to Canaan from Egypt unless he were completely lost; and if he were, it would take more miracles than Moses had to assure his survival. The peninsula of Sinai is a barren, arid waste of sand and rock, never inhabited by more than a few thousand half-starved Bedu. If Moses led the Hebrews there, one can hardly blame them for murmuring. No one would go there except to meet God—the reason alleged—and God can be met in more accessible places. The name of Sinai was not given to the present Sinai peninsula until the fourth century A.D. by Christian pilgrims. Later passages of the Bible suggest that by the eighth century B.C., the location of the mount of God was not known, and that the geography of the exodus is partly mythological.

In addition, scholars are reasonably assured that the body which Moses led was not the twelve tribes of Israel, as they are identified. We know that not all Americans had ancestors on the *Mayflower;* if we did not have the passenger list, we may suspect that the number of Mayflower families would be much larger than it is. The Priestly writer, probably in the fifth century B.C., calculated that Moses must have led an army of 600,000 men, which suggests a total population of 3,000,000. Since Thutmose III of Egypt conquered all of Canaan, and a good deal besides, in the fifteenth century B.C., with an army of 18,000 men (his own figures), one may calculate that a Hebrew host of this size would have caused an exodus of Egyptians rather than Hebrews. In any case, our problem of finding the identity of Moses is complicated by finding the identity of the group which he is said to have led out of Egypt.

The difficulty of locating Moses in time is greater than locating him in space. Those who think he can be dated place him in the middle of the thirteenth century B.C., not so much because of positive evidence as because there is no room for him elsewhere. This is not satisfactory. The period of Egyptian history called the New Kingdom is one of the better documented and dated periods of the ancient Near East. Scholars are compelled to place Moses just where this documentation becomes much less full, leading one to suspect that if we find out more about the period it will be difficult to locate Moses there too.

The problems of adjusting the story of Moses to what we know of history and geography suggest a limited acquaintance of the scribes with both history and geography. Narratives written without such information generally have a large component of imagination which, when applied to narrative, creates fiction. The theme of God as liberator of the oppressed is too important in the Old Testament to be easily dismissed as the work of fiction. Yet when the story of Moses as liberator is submitted to critical analysis it appears as a recital of the acts of God rather than as historical narrative. The scribes were not writing anyone's memories; they were writing a theological explanation of existing reality, and that reality was Israel the people of God. One must suppose they did not write memories because no memories existed.

I mention that the scribes had not only writings and folklore but cultic recitals and songs. One could hardly write the history of our War of 1812 from its most famous literary monument, "The Star Spangled Banner." I am not even sure that one could discover from the song that the battle mentioned took place at Baltimore—because like most Americans I do not know all the words. And one could never deduce from "The Star Spangled Banner" that the United States took a bad beating in the war. I suggest that the scribes had nothing but materials of this sort from which to construct their epic of Moses the liberator. With the material available we have simply no way in which to write a history of Moses as liberator; and I say this after looking at the effort of a colleague to write such a history in the *Encyclopedia Britannica*.

We may now turn to Moses as mediator and revealer.

Setting aside the laws, which we shall discuss separately, the main elements of the revelation of Moses are the revelation of the name of God, the identity of this God with the ancestral God, and the intention of this God to liberate his people and bring them into Canaan. The intention of God can be deduced from what actually happened in the story. The identity of the God revealed by Moses with the ancestral God cannot be achieved without establishing some artificial genealogies and some artificial narratives; we discussed this in an earlier chapter. The revelation of the name of God is attributed to Moses because no other claimant has appeared. It is not without interest that in answer to Moses' question about God's name, the answer in Exodus 3:14 does not give the name; where the name should stand there is a play on words. But the name is given in the following verse (probably compiled from a different source). Scholars read and pronounce the name as YAHWEH. Jews ceased to pronounce this name out of reverence in the second century B.C., and the pronunciation of the name was lost for hundreds of years.

In ancient Israel the name was important. Whether it was the name of a person or an object, it was supposed to tell one something about its bearer. Israelites meant more than we mean when they said that you do not know a person until you know his name. Knowledge of the name gave a certain power; kings were not addressed by name but by title, a circumlocution we still use for dignitaries. Not to know the name of a God was to have no dealings with him; it was to treat him as nothing. Thus the group to whom Moses spoke must have had a name for its god; unless the late W. F. Albright was right in thinking it was El Shaddai, the ancient name was not preserved.

The name told one how to address God and told one the

kind of god he was; for all Hebrew personal names have meaning, even though we do not always know it. The principle fails us for the name of God; we do not know what Yahweh means. If the name was meaningful in Israel, the meaning has been lost. An etymology as early as the Hebrew text connects it with the word "to be" in what is called the causative stem; thus the name would be associated with the idea "bring into being." More precision than this association is not possible within the grammatical framework of the name; and there have been at least a dozen modern efforts to interpret the name, none of them convincing.

The character of God is revealed less in the name than in the recital, as I have called it; he is the God of the oppressed. This is more than meets the eye. The ancient world had no gods of the oppressed. I am aware that gods in Mesopotamia and Egypt (and probably in Canaan, if we had the material) are called defenders of the poor and needy. We know that these gods (apart from the fact that they are not real) were owned and managed by the landowning aristocracy for whom they worked. One wonders whether the average peasant and craftsman in the ancient Near East was not a practical atheist. No one has ever doubted that Yahweh was the God of the oppressed as no other god was; the history of the religion of Israel showed that he resisted the ownership and management of the landowning aristocracy who tried to capture him as they have tried to own every god since land-ownership was invented. Only in our day has an attempt been made to submit him to the ownership and management of the oppressed.

This exposition, I hope, suggests that the story of Moses as the revealer of the God of the oppressed does not bristle with difficulties as the story of Moses the liberator does; to borrow a phrase from Voltaire, if Moses did not exist, we should have to invent him. The role of Moses as mediator of a covenant likewise, with reservations, does not offer the same problems. The problems arise from the fact that the covenant Moses is described as making on behalf of Israel has elements which scholars (again!) think must be later than Moses.

In the Pentateuch Moses is credited with the explicit foundation of nearly the entire Israelite legal and cultic system. Even the "tabernacle" is a tent built according to the dimensions of the temple of Solomon. The essence of the covenant relationship, stripped of later accretions, is that the relation of God and Israel is the result of free choice, an election made and accepted. It is like a marriage, which later prophets likened it to. Recent studies suggest that it is analogous to the treaties made between suzerains and vassals, in which the vassal accepted certain obligations in return for the assurance of powerful protection.

In Joshua 24 there is an account of how Joshua imposed a covenant with Yahweh upon the tribes of Israel. The covenant is called a renewal; the scribes obviously had the account of the covenant which was imposed upon Israel by Moses. The late Martin Noth noticed several details in the account which suggest that the covenant is not renewed but imposed upon a group for the first time. Those who are already worshipers of Yahweh are Joshua "and his house." One may conclude that this suggests that Joshua is more clearly a covenant mediator than Moses. The covenant of Joshua is quite simple, demanding no more than the exclusive worship of Yahweh. As we shall see shortly, the covenant of Moses is much more complex, and to that degree less credible. One may suggest that Moses, the founder, attracted to himself some of the acts not only of Joshua but of other later figures.

We may now turn to the role of Moses as lawgiver. Let us observe at once that the laws of the Pentateuch (counted by the rabbis as 613) are in the hypothesis of the suzerainty treaty the "stipulations" of the treaty, the list of obligations laid upon the vassal as a definition of his fidelity to his suzerain. In Joshua 24, on the other hand, the only stipulation is the renunciation of the worship of other gods and the worship of Yahweh alone. This becomes more closely defined in the laws of the Pentateuch; this stipulation, for instance, is the first two of the Ten Commandments. Observe that the Second Commandment makes explicit what is implicit in the covenant of Joshua, the prohibition of the adoration of images.

During the centuries in which the laws of the Pentateuch were the oldest laws known, much could be written about the advanced jurisprudence of the inspired lawgiver. Since the earliest of several collections discovered in Mesopotamia goes back to about 2000 B.C., we are able both to compare the jurisprudence of the inspired lawgiver with his uninspired predecessors and to see his dependence on these predecessors. Practically all the laws of Moses which are not directly religious have their antecedents in what may be called the common consuetudinary law of the ancient Near East. That the religious laws in content and formulation are not derived from these sources is important; with these we deal with original Israelite formulations. But do we deal with Moses?

Moses is described as the leader of a group of nomadic herdsmen. This itself raises questions, as we have seen; but if there is one thing clear about nomadic herdsmen, it is that they do not live by law. They are kinship groups or extended families; they have a family structure, not a political structure. Law is a product of civilization, indeed of urban civilization; it is quite safe to say that the group which Moses is described as leading did not have laws. This does not mean that kinship groups do not have rigid standards of conduct; they do. But they are not laws; they are family rules, and more often they are unspoken standards. A gentleman or a lady does not do things like that. How do you know what they are? If you are not a gentleman or a lady, no one can tell you. The Israelites could not have had laws until they became an urban civilization.

The question is apt why the laws were credited to Moses. The question is no more and no less the same question which is asked about other founders and lawmakers. Why should Lycurgus be a legendary lawmaker, or Numa Pompilius? Nothing is known of these legendary figures which entitles them to their status as lawgivers. In Israel we find that in the early phases of rabbinic scribalism there was a desire to attach several literary traditions to founders. David becomes the author of all psalms and Solomon the author of all wisdom. Neither of these attributions can be justified. So likewise Moses becomes the author of all law; neither can this attribution be justified. The laws of Israel, like the Pentateuch in which they are found, are the product of processes which endured for several hundred years; the authors are anonymous.

The reader may ask at this point whether I have not left the countenance of Moses veiled, as one story said that Moses was (to shield the Israelites from his glow, not from his horns). I can only say that it is not I who veiled the countenance of Moses, but the Israelite scribes. It is they who have given him his many faces, which we may not call masks. Where is the real Moses? He is no easier to find than the historical Jesus, who has given many scholars much anguish.

One must admit that Moses is a legendary figure, and in saying this one may have said everything. The legendary figure is not by definition unhistorical. But we may not know much about him that is historical. There may indeed have been a King Arthur of Britain. But the Arthur of Thomas Malory is unhistorical. The Arthur of Malory lived in Malory's time and culture; and Moses lived in the time and culture of the scribes who wrote about him.

To come nearer to our own times, Jesse James became a legend in his own time—a legend, I read, that he was careful to cultivate. The legend of Jesse James as a Robin Hood who robbed the rich to give to the poor is a lie any way you slice it. The historical reality of Jesse James was a psychopathic self-pitying killer who thought that anyone who had more than himself was a thief. I do not imply that the legend of Moses is of this quality, but I simply illustrate the formation of legend. The scribes did not distort the historical reality of Moses; like Thomas Malory, they had no historical reality to distort.

We are left, it seems, with a historical reality which is still veiled from our view. We may as well accept this; we can learn from Moses much about the Israel which produced this legendary figure, and what we can learn repays our study. It can be said that what people thought happened is often more important than what really happened. Moses is an excellent example of this. The belief that God is the liberator of the oppressed has been more meaningful than whatever it was that Moses did. I doubt whether anyone wants to propose that this belief is founded upon falsehood, particularly upon a false understanding of God.

# A KING LIKE ALL THE NATIONS

IN I Samuel 8:1-9 Samuel in his old age was approached by the elders of Israel with the request that he would give them a king like all the nations. Samuel prayed and was given a divine oracle: "They have not rejected you; they have rejected me as their king." The narrative of the institution of Israel's king continues through chapters 8-11 of I Samuel. Since Saul, the first king, was a failure, the institution of the monarchy was not solid until the election of David, anointed in I Samuel 16 and established king of all Israel in 2 Samuel 5. David thus became the founder of a dynasty which endured from about 960 B.C. to 587 B.C.—a long time as far as dynasties go.

The passage just quoted comes from the writer whom interpreters identify as the Deuteronomic historian. He is believed to be the author of a history which included all the books beginning with Deuteronomy and ending with 2 Kings in our present Bible. The purpose of this history is to show that the judgments of God on the kingdoms of Israel and Judah were altogether right and just. With this view of Israelite history as a whole, it is not surprising that his evaluation of the origins of the Israelite monarchy was hostile. This did not keep him from including stories of the origin of the monarchy which were favorable; such were the accounts of the election of Saul in I Samuel 9:1—10:16 and of the election of David in I Samuel 16. The ancient scribe often simply amassed his sources without arranging them. The hostile judgment of the historian was easily justified by the course of the history of the

Israelite monarchy; he treats it as vitiated in its very beginning, a rebellion against the kingship of God.

Recent studies have suggested—a suggestion not accepted by all scholars, perhaps not even by most—that the Israelite league of tribes formed in the land of Canaan by covenant with one God and with each other was a rejection of the social-political-theological system of the Canaanite city-states. The power in this system was centered in a king and a landowning military aristocracy. The gods of the city-state furnished the religious undergirding of this monopoly of power. The tenant peasants were simply exploited for the wealth of the ruling class. One has to believe that the Canaanite system was more exploitative than the Egyptian system, which was much more stable and by all indications gave the tenant peasants a greater share of the riches which they produced.

When one thinks of Israelite law as a reaction to the Canaanite system, a number of features become clear. Thus the Israelite law of retaining property within the family prevented the acquisition of large estates and the growth of a landowning aristocracy. There is no trace of a landed nobility in early Israel. Before Saul there was no king. The league of tribes was an apolitical union which had no power and did not govern. Government was local. The key words in the quoted phrase are "a king like all the nations," meaning a king on the Canaanite model.

Historians generally agree that the monarchy was a response to the Philistine movement into southwestern Canaan, a movement which gave the land its permanent name (Palestine). This Mediterranean people was a military aristocracy, superior to the Israelite peasants in arms and discipline. The stories of the origins of the monarchy are not without romance. Election falls upon Saul, a young man pursuing strayed livestock for his father and then upon David, still a shepherd boy. Historians, a critical lot, tend to take these stories about as seriously as the story of Arthur drawing Excalibur from the rock. Both Saul and David appear to have been what the Israelites wanted and thought they needed —warlords.

When I say that I wish someone would write the history of the mercenary soldier in the ancient Near East, I risk some letters from my colleagues referring me to some books already written. I will be grateful for the reference at the cost of some humiliation. Some years ago Moshe Greenberg wrote a monograph on the Habiru (or Hapiru), a social class (not an ethnic title) who appear over a thousand years of ancient Near Eastern history. They were often indentured servants and mercenary soldiers. This is the same word which comes to us through the Bible as Hebrew. It seems quite likely that both Saul and David were Habiru. I called them warlords. They can easily be likened to the warlords of Renaissance Italy and of modern China before World War II.

The "warlord" appears through most of recorded history. They are men who lead private armies; David is credited with a band of four hundred men "in distress and in debt and discontented" (I Samuel 22:2). The warlord hires his military strength out to the highest bidder. When the private army is temporarily unemployed, it lives off the country; the warlord becomes a bandit. In I Samuel 25 we read a clear case of extortion practiced by David, the same kind of extortion practiced by modern urban gangs against merchants. William the Conqueror was a descendant of the Norsemen and their waterborne private armies. Like David, he founded a kingdom.

Biblical stories of Saul and David show a reasonably clear picture of David, a lesser warlord, hiring himself and his band to Saul, a greater warlord. A quarrel between the two issued in private war which ultimately destroyed Saul and his house and delivered the kingdom to David—who had transferred his service from Saul to the enemies of Saul, the Philistines. David was recognized first by Judah then by Israel. When he felt strong enough, he rebelled against his overlords, the Philistines.

I remarked that the Canaanite polity had a theological undergirding which the Israelites rejected. It was a mark of the genius of David that he with his scribes was able to create a theological undergirding for his throne out of the very beliefs which rejected kingship as rebellion against God. Some of my colleagues refer to this as "the royal Jerusalem theology." It will appear below how large a place this theology has occupied in other books of the Old Testament and in Christian belief, and it is probably wise at this point to remark that the Deuteronomic historian was hostile to the Davidic dynasty and, presumably to the theology upon which it rested. In most ancient Near Eastern monarchies the king was the earthly plenipotentiary of the god who had established his throne and confirmed his power. Only in Egypt was the king himself a god. More subtlety was demanded to establish the Israelite king as the plenipotentiary of the Israelite god.

The theological task was accomplished simply by moving David into position between God and Israel. The relations between God and Israel were not changed; but God did not reach Israel except through David, nor did Israel reach God except through David. God chose David as king (and not merely to rule Israel; words become important here); this is the point of the story in I Samuel 16. God chose a man whom he empowered to rule; and this is the point of the anointing in the same chapter. Anointing was the rite by which the spirit of God was conferred as a permanent possession. The stories of such early heroes as Gideon, Jephthah and Samson told how the spirit of God seized and moved them to deeds of heroism by which Israel was saved. This spirit, the principle of wisdom and strength, now reposed permanently upon the king and empowered him to execute the two functions of kingship—war and law. It is not without interest that in the Deuteronomic historian's account of the accession of Saul, the king is chosen by lot and he is not anointed.

The election and the charismatic spirit justify the interposition of David into the covenant of God with Israel. This becomes a covenant of God with David and through David with Israel; this is the point of the oracle in 2 Samuel 7. The covenant with David is assured by the pledge of an eternal dynasty. Israel cannot fall because God has promised that David will stand. Obviously, some theological dexterity was required to cope with the fall of the dynasty of David in 587 B.C.

David appears to have had the virtues expected in a bandit chieftain, and one of these is shrewdness. Whether he himself initiated the social changes in Israel which occurred under his successor is not clear. It is clear that with Solomon the kingship returned to the Canaanite polity described above, noted in particular by the scribe who quoted Rehoboam as saying that his father had chastised the Israelites with whips, but he would chastise them with scorpions (I Kings 12:1-11). As a response to Solomon's policy what had formerly been Israel seceded from the Jerusalem dynasty never to return.

The motive for this rebellion is defined by the scribes as forced labor—the same feature of ancient society from which, in Israelite traditions, Moses liberated the Israelite forefathers. The quality of life under the monarchy is attested by the prophets Amos, Hosea, Isaiah, Micah and Jeremiah. One sees in these books the rise of a ruling landlord class under royal patronage; the king had no way to reward his servants except by the donation of other people's land. We read of the corruption of legal processes by bribery and the use of illegal methods to extort their possessions from the poor. We read of a peasant class perpetually in debt and sliding from debt into slavery. These appear to be the very qualities of life in the Canaanite city-states which led the Israelites to reject that life for a new system in which they trusted in God the Liberator. Now God the Liberator was enshrined in a little temple which was an annex to the palace of the king, the great landlord. The Israelites had what they had desired, a king like all the nations. By any standards, whether the secular standards of success in politics and the production of prosperity, or the religious standards of moral integrity in government and in civil life, the monarchy was a ghastly failure.

I remarked earlier that the collapse of the Davidic monarchy caused serious concern to the scribes of Judaism who preserved the promise of an eternal dynasty to David. We must now return to the theory that the king possessed the spirit of God as a permanent gift. He received the spirit by anointing; he was the "anointed," which comes into English through the transcription of the Hebrew word as Messiah. The word came into Greek as *christos,* then into English as Christ. David was Messiah, and so were each of his successors. Psalm 72 illustrates the qualities which the Jerusalem king should exhibit as Messiah. He has the wisdom necessary to govern through law, and the courage to defend his people against aggression. Solomon, who seems to have been in fact one of the greatest fools ever to wield political power, somehow acquired a reputation for wisdom, illustrated in his judgment of the two prostitutes and their children.

The Messiah had to have wisdom in an eminent degree. The unrealism of this theology seems apparent to us when we review the sorry list of the shallow bunglers who sat on the throne of David; how could it survive? It survived, it seems, because there was always hope that the spirit would work in the successor what it had not worked in his predecessor. The accession of a king who received the spirit at his anointing was always a pledge of hope.

But the dynasty did fall with no prospect of revival. The promise of the eternal dynasty could be fulfilled only in a restoration. The hope—indeed the assurance—of a restoration appears in late books of the Old Testament and even more clearly in some extrabiblical Jewish writings. From these arise the "messianic hope" of which commentators on the New Testament speak. The hope was that the dynasty and power of David would be restored by a descendant of David who would be all that a charismatic king ought to be—a David rather than his lightweight successors. That the descendant should exhibit the character of David, the ideal king, shows to what a degree the thug who was the historical David had been overlaid with plaster. And it should be clearly understood that the Messiah King Savior who was expected was no more of a spiritual force than David himself had been. He was expected to liberate Jews from the yoke of the Gentile oppressors and restore to them the world dominion which was their right—simply because no one else had a right to it. The Messiah King Savior was expected to be a political and military hero.

With this view of "popular" messianism current in New

Testament times (as if there were any other kind), it is some-what strange that the early disciples of Jesus gave him this title, turning the Hebrew Messiah into the Greek Christ when the gospel was proclaimed to Gentiles. Students of the Gospels are convinced that Jesus himself neither claimed nor accepted the title, and presented himself in no way as a political or military hero. He did not urge the poor to arise against their oppressors nor did he move in any way toward insurrection against Rome. He was executed on a charge of sedition against Rome which historians are satisfied was false.

The disciples gave Jesus the title of Messiah because there was no other title correct in Jewish belief which defined his role. The title Messiah did not define it either; the role of Jesus is unique and can be described in no known categories. Paul, writing mostly to Gentiles, preferred the title of Lord—a political title also in Roman Hellenism, but not open to the misconceptions of popular Jewish messianism. Furthermore, the lordship of Jesus was not to be fully established before the eschatological end of days. And the disciples effectively trans-formed the idea of messianism when they gave the title to Jesus. They recognized that he was not and never claimed to be a political savior. By affirming that Jesus was Messiah they denied that the Jews could ever expect the conquering hero, the scion of David, to arise.

As he is described in the Gospels, Jesus was as nonpolitical as anyone could desire. A few recent efforts to identify him with the Jewish faction called Zealots—freedom fighters or guerrilla bandits of the time, depending on one's point of view—have not been judged successful by scholars. In all the collected sayings of Jesus available to the early church the Christian scribes could find only one saying touching politics: "Render to Caesar what belongs to Caesar, and to God what belongs to God." Christian interpreters, anguished that Jesus showed no interest in politics, have attempted to erect a political philosophy upon this saying. It is clear to anyone who reads the passage that Jesus refused to answer the question which was asked about the morality of paying taxes to the imperial government of Rome. This was a sticky question in Palestinian Judaism, something like asking a modern Palestinian Arab whether he should pay taxes to the Israeli government. The answer of Jesus is to return the question to the personal decision of those who asked it, adding that the use of coined money is itself a recognition of the legitimacy of the government which issues the money.

It may be observed that Jesus was a member of that class called in the Gospels the poor or the meek or those who hunger and thirst for righteousness; this numbers him among that great silent majority of the poor of the Roman world who were politically inactive because they were powerless. He did not speak, one may say, to the citizens of the modern western democratic states who are at least constitutionally able to determine their own destiny. One may respond that the political powerlessness of the majority did not deter many Palestinian villagers from taking part in that political activity which was available to them, the terrorism of the Zealots; but this is not really the point.

The point here is that Jesus never suggested that the Good News which he proclaimed would be realized by any political means, then or later. The salvation which Jesus revealed could be attained without any modification in political and social structures. Political and social changes could not advance this salvation; neither could they retard it. When Jesus called the poor happy, possibly one of the things he implied was that wealth gives no one an edge in the pursuit of the essential salvation. Not all of those who profess belief in him have accepted this implication.

It is, of course, paradoxical that we can close this chapter with the text with which we began it. It is discouraging when one reflects how often in the last sixteen hundred years the churches which call themselves Christian and the members of those churches have asked for a king like all the nations. I say the last sixteen hundred years rather than the last two thousand. Until Constantine issued the Edict of Milan in 313 the Christians were like the poor and the meek of the Gospels, politically powerless. It seemed that almost suddenly the Roman Empire became Christian. At the same time the church became Roman. Gibbon, the historian of the Roman Empire, said that this destroyed the Roman Empire, and he was almost right. The ethos of the Roman Empire should not have been able to survive under Christian management.

What Gibbon failed to realize, however, was how much of the Roman ethos Christians learned to live with. By their acceptance of the Roman ethos the church was compromised in its Christianity to a degree from which it has not yet fully recovered. Since Constantine the churches and their members have believed that political power and political means can and ought to be used to promote the interests of the church. Jesus and the first Christians did not employ these means not because they were inept for the purposes of the church, but simply because they did not have them. When they became available, they were a gift of God to the needy. Among other sayings of Jesus conveniently forgotten was the saying that if he had wanted twelve legions of angels he could have had them. He might have refused the legions of angels, but his successors have never refused the offer of quite human legions, and have often felt helpless when neither angelic nor human legions were at hand.

And what were the interests of the church which political means supported and advanced? They were the same interests which political means support in political societies. They include the acquisition and retention of landed property, the erection and maintenance of buildings, the accumulation of invested wealth and the protection of the revenues derived from it, and that without which none of these can be secure, the power to impose the will of the church on others. Can one fail to observe that Jesus makes explicit the renunciation of each of the items mentioned as a condition of membership in the Reign of God? Can one fail to notice that the work of our redemption was accomplished without these resources? The role of King Messiah Savior, rejected by Jesus, has been gladly accepted by those who carry on his mission.

Politics, like alcohol and narcotics, is addictive. The modern church has been effectively expelled from politics— for the wrong reasons, no doubt, but that may be unimportant; Jesus was killed for the wrong reasons. It is pathetic to see ministers of his church scratching for the kind of power possessed in abundance by the ward boss of a big city— meaningful enough, but even Chicago's mayor Richard J. Daley never claimed he could summon twelve legions of angels. The church in its addiction for politics seems never as a body to have realized that political power can be acquired only at a great price—often enough a man's soul, which, often enough, has been exacted from the church.

There are still those who believe that the reign of God will be effected not only by the conversion of men to God but by social engineering enacted into law. What Jesus did not accomplish by his death and resurrection will be accomplished by act of Congress. If Jesus had intended to achieve his objectives by legal acts, he had only to remain what many thought he was—a Pharisee.

# 10

## SO SAID THE LORD

IN the books of the Old Testament some religious figures appear which have no parallel elsewhere in the ancient world. The Hebrew word which designates them is translated into English as prophet. That they are without parallel elsewhere makes it difficult to analyze them; but the Old Testament also is quite obscure on their origins. They first appear surely in the tenth or eleventh centuries B.C.; they disappear after the fifth century. The English word prophet usually means one who foretells the future; this is so inadequate a description of the Israelite prophets that it is better not to think of them in these terms.

The Hebrew Bible has fifteen books which bear the names of prophets; the Greek and Latin Bibles have seventeen. The connection between the names and the books is often uncertain; it is certain that far more than fifteen or seventeen men were engaged in the production of these books. In addition to the prophetic books prophets are mentioned, often by name, in the stories of the kings of Israel and Judah. The best known of such prophets are Elijah and Elisha.

The best way to describe these figures is as spokesmen of God. They prefaced their sayings with a phrase like "Hear the word of the Lord" and concluded them with phrases like, "So said the Lord" or "The oracle of the Lord." These phrases, which serve as quotation marks, enclose sayings in which the first person is used to designate God as speaker. It is exactly the form of the letter delivered orally by a messenger, who identifies the sender and then speaks in the person of the sender. The ability to speak the word of God was a recognized charisma in Israel, ranked in Jeremiah 18:18 with the instruction of the priest and the counsel of the sage. It was very probably a skill learned from its possessors, like the instruction of the priest and the counsel of the sage.

Groups called "the sons of the prophets" appear in early Israel, probably in the tenth century B.C. These groups have nothing in common with the later prophets except the name, and it is not clear what the designation "sons of the prophets" means. Wherever they appear in the earliest incidents, they appear as groups of men who practice pentecostal rites of worship; vigorous dancing is mentioned, and song was probably included. Through these rites, it appears, they cultivated a type of religious exaltation which is a common pattern in religious experience. Were they no more than religious enthusiasts, they would present no problem.

Elijah and Elisha exhibit associations with such groups and some elements of exaltation in their own religious experience, as they are described in the sources. Certainly the wearing of a cloak of hair (Elijah) was a clear effort to establish some symbolic character; and it is this cloak which is said to have fallen upon Elisha when Elijah was rapt up in the fiery chariot. The historian concludes soberly that the story at least suggests that Elisha also wore this outlandish but clearly identifying garb.

Between the enthusiasts of the books of Samuel and the prophets of the prophetic books there is no clear connection. Elijah and Elisha admonished kings and threatened judgment, and these elements they have in common with the prophets of the books. The ideas of most scholars, I think, can be summed up as a gradual smoothing of religious practices which were originally harsh and uncouth. In this development the end product has almost nothing obviously in common with the first representatives. Possibly there was no such development. Amos, the first of the prophets, denied that he was a prophet or a son of a prophet, meaning a member of the worship groups (Amos 7:14). His denial of community with the "prophets" has not been taken seriously except by the Hebrew scribes who edited the books of the prophets, and attached the designation prophet to none of them in the title except the postexilic prophets Haggai and Zechariah.

As far as I know, no one has suggested that the word "prophet" was misapplied to the prophets of the prophetic books, and that the term had become somewhat derisive. When one of "the sons of the prophets" went to anoint Jehu as king of Israel, one of Jehu's officers called him a madman (2 Kings 9:11). But when the officers heard what the madman had done, they took him seriously enough and acclaimed Jehu as king. One suspects that the prophets, like most religious figures, elicited mixed reactions from men of the world.

It appears that the life of Jeremiah was spared from direct murder because of a superstitious fear of attacking the person of a prophet; and such fear was no token of belief (Jeremiah 38). The chief priest of Bethel ordered Amos out of the sanctuary because it was royal property (Amos 7:12-13). For threatening the temple itself Jeremiah was flogged and placed under restraint for a night (Jeremiah 20:1-2). Superstitious fear did not save the life of a prophet named Uriah, a contemporary of Jeremiah (Jeremiah 26:20-23); the author candidly says that Jeremiah escaped death only because of friends in high office. We have not too many instances of such personal attacks upon prophets.

The figures of Elijah and Elisha had already become legendary when their stories were compiled as we have them in 1-2 Kings, but the narrative discloses them as dedicated to the exclusive worship of Yahweh and in deadly opposition to the cult of the Canaanite Baal sponsored by the monarchy of the kingdom of Israel. The narrative also candidly reports the conspiracy and assassinations fostered by Elisha; those to whom religion is supremely important have often felt that there can be no immoral means to protect it against its enemies. It probably means, more than anything we have yet seen, that earlier prophets, with the exception of Gad and Nathan, the court prophets of David, appear in opposition to the monarchy.

We pointed out in an earlier chapter that the institution of the monarchy was regarded by many as a betrayal of the original faith and traditions of Israel. Gad and Nathan appear as officers of David's court, professional prophets who at request might deliver the word of God. Nathan, however, is the hero of the story of the rebuke of David for adultery and murder (2 Samuel 12), which is not the kind of oracle delivered in answer to the requests of kings. In this incident, and perhaps only in this one, can we find in the early prophets some foreshadowing of the prophets of the prophetic books.

I have observed that prophecy was probably a professional skill which we acquired like other professional skills, by living and studying with recognized masters of the skill. Among the prophets are included such men as Samuel, upon whom has been superimposed some features of the later prophets. He does appear as a village seer who among other skills (we suppose; they are not mentioned) could tell the owner of livestock where to look for stray animals. We also have the example of Elisha, who at least in one instance needed the stimulation of music to hear the word of God (2 Kings 3). The music does suggest a deliberately induced trance in which the prophet was endowed with clairvoyance; the name "seer" applied to prophets also suggests this. The cultivation of such ecstatic trances appears to be a part of the professional technique of prophets.

Such professional skill is not characteristic of the prophets of the books. The denial of Amos that he was a prophet implies both the existence of a professional class and his own non-membership in such a class. He is a prophet, he says, because God called him to prophesy. "Vocation" narratives are also found for Isaiah (Isaiah 6) and Jeremiah (Jeremiah 1:4-10). Jeremiah is explicit that the kind of vocation he experienced was not experienced by those whom he calls "prophets"; they spoke of their own volition and not under the impulse which he felt, of which we shall say more below. We do not know the basis of Jeremiah's assurance that he alone had such a call, and possibly it is simply that no one else made such a claim. If prophecy was a professional skill, no such claim was necessary.

The prophetic experience is most frequently described as hearing the word of God, which the prophet then repeats. This is a figure of speech for an experience which cannot be described directly because there is no analogy to it in ordinary experience. That I, for example, have not had the mystical experience does not entitle me to deny that anyone had it; that would be like the tone-deaf person saying that two thousand people who listen to an orchestra playing a symphony are engaging in a vast pretense. No discussion of the prophetic experience can proceed without the assumption that the prophets experienced God in a way which the vast majority of us do not share. Jeremiah described the experience of the word of God as a fire within him which pained him until he vented it (Jeremiah 20:9).

Of all the prophets, Jeremiah tells us most about the prophetic experiences, and perhaps we should not too rashly extend his experience to others, who show none of the resistance which Jeremiah offered to the word of God nor any of the anguish which he felt because the word set him in opposition to almost all of his own people. I say "almost," because the book, as we have seen, shows that Jeremiah had friends in high places. It shows also that he took no pleasure in announcing the impending destruction of his world. The prophet Hosea apparently first recognized the word of God in a shattering personal experience of the infidelity of his wife. Isaiah seems to have heard the word in an insight into the holiness of God which repels wickedness like a consuming fire. Amos said simply that God told him to go. None of these men shows any of the doubts and hesitation which Jeremiah never entirely overcame. And from these doubts there arose the question, which he alone raises, of true and false prophecy.

The collection of sayings in Jeremiah 23:9-40 is assembled around the theme of lying prophets. They are liars, Jeremiah says, because they speak for God without a commission. What they call "the word of God" is simply the product of their own minds or their dreams. This again may be Jeremiah's way of distinguishing his own inner compulsion from the techniques of professional prophecy. The reference of visions and dreams suggests the skills of autohypnosis. The encounter of prophet with prophet is illustrated in the encounter of Jeremiah and Hananiah (Jeremiah 28). Shortly before, Jeremiah had made himself a miniature yoke which he wore as a prophetic symbol of the yoke of Babylon (Jeremiah 27). Such a technique was probably borrowed from the repertory of professional prophetic skills. Hananiah, who predicted deliverance within two years, responded to one symbol with another; he broke the yoke which Jeremiah was wearing.

At the moment Jeremiah had no response. His words to Hananiah lack the assurance which we expect him to have, and which appears in a response delivered some time later. Certainly Jeremiah did not have the word of God on demand; and the anecdote illustrates the doubt and uncertainty which plagued the prophet—and which did not appear in the conduct of Hananiah. Jeremiah did not question the sincerity of Hananiah. In Hebrew the "lie" is an untruth, whether sincerely spoken or not; the language did not distinguish between mendacity and misinformation. But Jeremiah approaches the distinction when he charges the prophets with announcing good news instead of the truth, which is bad news (Jeremiah 6:14—8:11; 23:17). This is to encourage evildoers by not warning them of the consequences of their evil deeds (Jeremiah 23:14).

We have included among professional prophets what are called court prophets such as Gad and Nathan, who seem to have been cabinet officers of David, and the four hundred prophets whom Ahab could summon to predict victory (I Kings 22). It is doubtful that Ahab retained a staff of this number, although there is no doubt that they announced what the king wanted to hear and therefore lived off the royal bounty. Some scholars have proposed that the temple also had professional prophets who spoke the word of God in the liturgy. Such prophets belonged to the religious and political establishment of Israel, which they served.

The prophets of the books did not belong to the establishment and can hardly be called a religious institution. The vocations which we have mentioned were vocations of individual men and there is no evidence that the office was passed to another or that there was a succession of prophets. When the wife of Isaiah is called a prophetess, this means no more than "Mrs. Prophet." The prophets not only stood outside the institutions, they were usually hostile to them. I think that to announce that an institution is doomed to imminent destruction because of its total religious and moral corruption expresses a degree of hostility. It is not what modern political and religious institutions would regard as constructive criticism.

The prophets could not have spoken in these terms if they had not made themselves independent of the institutions which dictated the terms in which the lying prophets of Jeremiah were to speak. It is difficult for members of the modern institutional church, which is far more closely organized and administered than the religion of the Israelite monarchies was, to grasp the fact that the spokesmen of God had to stand outside the institution and against it. The institution by its nature smothers criticism. Because the prophets stood outside the organization they have no successors in the institutional structure of the modern church, which tolerates prophetic speech about as cordially as the Pharisees and the Sadducees tolerated the prophetic speech of Jesus.

Thus we are driven back to the assurance—in spite of such doubts as those of Jeremiah—with which these men spoke what they said was the word of God. This assurance, I said, must have a mystical base which ultimately defies analysis; but the prophets have left a few clues about the experience. We must explain before giving some illustrations that the ancient world had beliefs about the existence and power of the spoken word which we do not share. To utter a word was to produce a reality which remained in existence until it reached its fulfillment. And one never really knew when fulfillment was reached; the word did not have inexhaustible meaning, but there was always the possibility that it meant more than you heard it say. And since the power of the word was measured by the power of the speaker, obviously the power of the word of God was beyond measure. When God speaks, he creates.

Now we turn to the visions of Amos (Amos 7:1—8:4). In the early prophets the vision is a much rarer literary form than in the later prophets; and it is, as here in Amos, an imaginary vision, a poetic image. We begin with the last, the vision of the basket of fruit. Amos sees a basket (*qayis*); what the basket shows him is the *end* (*qes*) of Israel. The two words may have been pronounced alike in the eighth century. Here is the force of the word when spoken by God; it has its full force. No mystic vision is implied; Amos could have seen a basket of fruit in the marketplace. The word of God is the basket, which tells him certainly that the end is here. You cannot do this in English.

The other visions are also objects in nature or experience. The word of God is in the word-thing which Amos sees— locusts, fire (probably drought), obvious symbols of destruction. The man with the plumb line used the tool by which ancient masons determined whether the wall stood straight or was so far out of line that it had to be demolished. God has laid the plumb line against Israel and decided that it must be demolished. And the sight of the altar (Amos 9:1) shows him God standing beside it ordering the demolition of the temple.

There are two similar visions in Jeremiah 1:11-14 which illustrate the explosive meaning of the word-thing when God utters the word by revealing the thing. Again we are dealing with objects of experience, not of mystical vision. The first is an almond twig (*shaqed*). The almond was called *shaqed* (waker) because of its early blossoms. Behind the almond is the Awake One, the Watcher (*shoqed*), God, vigilant to fulfill his word—in this case his threats. The second object is a boiling pot to the north of Jeremiah, tipped and about to spill its content to the south. The route from the north down the coast of Phoenicia was the traditional route of invading armies from Mesopotamia. In the word-thing which Jeremiah observes the word of God is heard.

The word of God came to Hosea not in observing objects in nature and experience but in a personal tragedy. His wife was unfaithful and it seems he could not bring himself to reject her as the law not only permitted but demanded. The insight was that this is the experience of God with Israel. So far God seeks reconciliation and forgiveness rather than the strict processes of law. Hosea's vision of God certainly reflects Hosea's own softheartedness, just as Amos' vision of God reflects Amos' own rugged sense of justice. Yet both come to the same conclusion, an unmitigated sentence of doom. Hosea transfers to God his own sense of outrage pushed past the point of tolerance.

What is called the inaugural vision of (Isaiah 6) occurred in the temple of Jerusalem. The prophet uses imaginative symbols of a sudden awareness of the near presence of God; he is describing a mystical experience. The seraphs from other biblical allusions may be personifications of the tongues of flame, the heavenly fire which appeared whenever God was visibly manifested. The experience was an insight into the reality described by the Hebrew word which we translate "holy." The idea of the holy is as old as religion itself; it designates that area where the deity is believed to be present and active in a peculiar way in which he is not experienced elsewhere. Persons and objects which belong to this area share in the holiness of the area. The book of Leviticus is an example of the rules which regulate entrance into the holy place and fitting conduct within it. The insight of Isaiah seems to have been that the holiness of God abhors sin much more profoundly than it abhors ritual profanation. His response is a cry of despair; he is lost and the people among whom he lives are lost because they cannot withstand the presence of holiness. The word which arises from this insight is a threat of total destruction. What Isaiah actually saw was the temple, which in his day still housed the ark, the throne of God.

The prophetic word may be seen as a formulation of the prophet's basic insight into the reality of God, perhaps one such experience so rich that it is capable of indefinite variety of formulation. Outside of certain formulae of introduction and conclusion, there does not seem to be any particularly "prophetic" literary form. Modern literary studies find that the prophets use many forms of expression, all of which appear to have their origin in the secular and religious life of Israel. Isaiah (Isaiah 5) uses a love song to express a prophetic saying. Amos (Amos 5:2) uses the funeral lament. The most common form is the legal plea, the form which was used to bring a charge in court. However obscure the prophets may be to modern readers, they reflect the thought and speech of ordinary life of ancient Israel. Like the Gospels, their imagery is drawn from the same ordinary life, about which it tells us much. The prophets were men of the people who spoke to the people.

# 11

## SAVE BY DESTROYING

IN a book I published on the Old Testament twenty years ago I referred to the process of judgment in the Old Testament prophets as God saving his people by destroying them. Some readers thought that this phrase approached the limit of the tolerable in paradox, if it did not actually transgress it. I was not amused when, during the Vietnam war over ten years ago, an American officer said to some reporters that the Army had no way to save a certain village except by destroying it. I do not think this officer was one of my readers. He meant, of course, that the village was saved from falling into the hands of the enemy; most people thought this was a loose use of the word "save." I meant that God could save—that is, preserve—the religious and moral integrity of his people as well as the mission for which they were destined only by destroying the political and social structures in which they lived. Perhaps this also is a loose use of the word "save."

The serious reader of the Old Testament prophets soon finds the prevailing themes to be rather gloomy. There is more than a sufficiency of moral rebukes and threats of judgment. These elements are occasionally interrupted by promises of a glorious future of peace and prosperity under God's protection. The reader who has been through enough of the books will not be surprised to learn that many scholars years ago contrived the theory that the preexilic prophets spoke of nothing but the judgment which threatened the kingdoms of Israel and Judah; the promises, they thought, were added by later scribes who believed that the people of

121

God could look to more of a future than the prophets of doom gave them.

These rays of light were usually placed at the end of a literary collection which no longer appears as such in our Bibles. This was done on the scribal principle of the "happy ending." A work should not end on a note of unrelieved gloom. Thus 2 Kings, which probably first ended with the destruction of Jerusalem and chaos in the land of Judah, now ends with the note that there was a survivor of the dynasty of David living in Babylon. The book of Amos ended in the middle of 9:8 with God's word that he would utterly destroy the sinful kingdom, removing it from the face of the earth. The second half of verse 8 and all that follows contradicts this statement and promises a glorious future restoration.

Biblical critics no longer like such categorical statements which by definition make all oracles of promise postexilic; they prefer to settle each case on its own merits. In fact the merits of each case establish a weighty probability that the promises were later additions. My own thinking for some years has been that I am sure that Amos, Hosea and Jeremiah saw no future for the people whose end they announced. Israel had failed and God would work his will through some other people. I am aware that the argument is more difficult for Jeremiah. I feel less certain about Isaiah; this means that there are certain themes in Isaiah which I have not satisfactorily explained to myself. The possibility that Isaiah himself was ambiguous in the sense that his own thinking changed is serious, but we cannot reconstruct the development of his ideas on the kind of evidence we have. I would illustrate these three prophets by what is called the Deuteronomic history, the work which includes the books from Deuteronomy to Kings, quoted above as being enriched by a happy ending.

The Deuteronomic history can have had no other purpose than to show that God's judgments upon Israel and Judah were right and just; and the historian ends his work with this conviction.

Such a total view of judgment is not shared by all my colleagues, even for these four books. I can hardly use my phrase "save by destroying" (which really means salvation through judgment) of these books. They express, I am sure, the belief that God has totally and finally rejected Israel. Since there was an Israel which survived, even an Israel of somewhat tenuous continuity with the past, the view of the earlier prophets could hardly be maintained. We can understand why glosses of promise and "happy endings" were added to books like these. Jeremiah wrote as if he thought not only that repentance was impossible, but that even repentance would not alter the process of judgment which Israel had set in motion.

St. Paul did not understand the preexilic prophets; it is only fair to point out that modern criticism has turned up a large number of pieces of information which Paul did not have. He wrote in Romans 11:29 that the gifts and the call of God are irrevocable. He did not deal with the refusal of the Jews to accept Jesus Messiah as Amos and Jeremiah dealt with the refusal of their contemporaries to accept the salvation which God offered. Yet Paul is the chief witness in the New Testament to the Christian belief that the destiny of Israel is fulfilled in the Gentiles, although he was reared in the postexilic Jewish dogma of the indestructibility of Israel. It seems to me that precisely what Amos, Hosea, Isaiah (for at least part of his life) and Jeremiah addressed was an early form of this dogma.

Whether one accepts this understanding of the major

preexilic prophets or not, no one doubts that they announced, with or without a promised restoration, a catastrophic disaster of the society in which they lived. A disaster of such magnitude could not be expected to be reversed quickly in the normal course of history; what became of the Assyrians, the Moabites, the Edomites, and other neighbors of Israel? For the people whom the prophets addressed it was the end of their world; and this can be understood only by those who have seen their world end, like millions of Europeans in 1945.

If there had been prophets in western Europe who had announced the future in 1935—and there were those who feared it—and that what was going to happen was a righteous and just judgment of God on an entirely deserving people, I doubt that they would have been received with as little violence as the Israelite prophets suffered. They would be compelled to present some justification for the harsh judgment which they proclaimed. And it may be worth a few lines to explore the harshness of that judgment, which was defeat in wars in which the enemy was identified as the rod of God's wrath.

For sheer inhumanity as well as for the scale of human damage modern war makes ancient war look pallid. Modern war afflicts noncombatants not only more sorely than ancient war but more than it afflicts modern military men. Even after Word Wars I and II the American Civil War still leads the funeral parade of military casualities. But where ancient war destroyed Jerusalem, not much more than a village, modern weapons even in the hands of guerrilla warriors are destroying Beirut, a city of 250,000. One can hardly live in any neighborhood in a city like Chicago without having as neighbors some people whose world ended five thousand miles away in 1945 and who have no living relatives. Granted that modern civilization has achieved skills of killing and torturing which the Assyrians would envy, let us be sure that ancient war was no game of tag.

Ancient cities were not of a size or solidarity which made it difficult to destroy them so that, in the words of Jesus, not one stone remained upon another. Destruction, of course, meant displacement, but this was already planned. In ancient warfare the most valuable form of war booty was persons. Prisoners of war were the principal source of slaves, basic to the ancient economy; and it is hard at this distance to tell how many ancient wars were really slave raids. Women, of course, were helpless with the victors. Even Israelite law (Deuteronomy (21:10-14) has a provision for the treatment of women prisoners of war which was probably quite humane for the ancient world.

But before we exclaim in horror let those of us who are old enough remember what happened in the wars in Europe, Korea and Vietnam. For the defeated in ancient war it was, as I called it, the end of their world as totally as it is in modern war. Impoverishment and forcible displacement to another country was the easiest fare one could hope for. The reader who has access to reference works like James B. Pritchard's *Ancient Near East In Pictures* is recommended to consult the reproductions of the ancient Assyrian relief sculptures representing their own victories. It is probably the clearest commentary on the threats of the Israelite prophets.

How did one justify such threats? The prophets have often been called social critics, which is a flaccid designation. As I remarked above, one who announces the certain end of a society because it does not deserve to survive is engaging in more than social criticism. In an earlier chapter I observed that the dynasty of David and its schismatic successors in Israel restored the Canaanite model of kingship. They also restored the Canaanite model of society. Now exploitation of peasants by landlords has been a feature of the human community as far back as history goes and probably back to the first man who discovered that it was more profitable to own the land turned by the plow than to plow; and I suspect this was the man who invented the plow. Many voices have been raised against this exploitation; and it is even more remarkable how many voices have not been raised. But among the voices most loud and clear are the voices of the Israelite prophets.

Rather than summarize or paraphrase their words I recommend that the reader hear them firsthand. You may read Amos 2:6-8; 4:1-3; 5:10-13; 6:4-7; 8:4-6; Isaiah 3:13-15; 5:8-12; 10:1-4; Jeremiah 5:26-29. If you care to search for others besides this sampling, you will have no trouble finding them. You will recognize an oppressive ruling class which uses the entire resources of a country to enrich itself. You will see that the ruling class is identified with the government, that it has captured the legal processes, both of lawmaking and adjudication. You will observe that it has complete control over the religious institutions, which regularly celebrate the divine institution of the dynasty which is the creator and the patron of the landlord class.

Several of the prophets describe the society as lawless and, in terms which sound strangely prophetic to the inhabitant of modern large cities, say that no one is safe even in pursuing the ordinary business of life. The ruling class which plunders those whom it rules is hostile to others who plunder its victims only when they deprive the ruling class of its gains. Jeremiah describes a society in which mutual trust has broken down, and one does not know whether the person to whom one speaks can be expected to tell the truth. It is a society in which everyone, as he describes it, is looking for what in modern times is called the edge. Every transaction is governed by the mutual desire to extract more profit than the transaction legitimately permits. A breakdown of the mutual trust which enables one to ask a stranger for directions without worrying whether the stranger from sheer meanness will send one in the opposite direction is more than a breakdown of law; it is a breakdown of basic human relations. One wonders whether Jeremiah is not exaggerating; and one is forced to admit that he was there.

The prophets pay less attention to sexual sin than most modern prophets have done. This is not to say that they ignore it. The word adultery occurs frequently in their reproaches. The fact that Hosea and Jeremiah use adultery as the metaphor to describe the infidelity of Israel to God does not show tolerance for sexual aberrations. But there is a religious motif implied in sexual sin which is not immediately apparent to the modern reader. Ritual prostitution was a universal part of the religions of the ancient Near East. This practice was a part of the fertility rites which, it seems, were characteristic of the celebration of the New Year. Thus when the prophets speak of sexual licentiousness they mean more than we mean. It is thought that some such practice lies behind the indignation of Amos in 2:7. The indignation of the prophets is directed less at unchastity than against a religion which destroys any esteem for chastity.

When one reviews the prophetic books which are most read and studied, one observes that Amos, Micah and Isaiah are more concerned with the breakdown of society; Hosea, Jeremiah and Ezekiel were more concerned with the break-

down of religion. This is a very rough generalization which
shows differences of emphasis. The failure of society and the
failure of religion appear in all the prophets; and all of them
agree that the failure of society is an effect of the failure of
religion. The people are destroyed because of lack of knowledge (Hosea 4:6), the knowledge which it was the duty of the
priest to teach. Jeremiah (8:8) said that the lying pen of the
scribes had turned the law of the Lord into a lie. Whether
Isaiah 28:7-8 speaks properly of intoxication as a typical vice
of the priests or uses the figure of intoxication to denote
uncertainty, he certainly means that priests and prophets fail
to deliver vision (the charisma of the prophet) and judgment
(the charisma of the priest).

A Canaanite society could only be founded upon a
Canaanite theology. This generalization is valid for ancient
culture; it is not valid for modern culture. The modern society
is candidly worldly, and it is the society which creates the
theology it believes it needs. In most of western society it has
created a tame theology which will not disturb its secular
pursuits and methods. Modern society, "Christendom," has
not yet, except in Marxist countries, been able to bring itself to
say that what it really wants is no theology. Whether western
society has produced an updated version of Canaanite theology is an interesting question which I raise but shall not
pursue here.

In the ancient world it was believed—sincerely, as far as we
can tell—that no human activity could be conducted without
a theological basis which determined the activity to be one
thing or another. Society did not produce theology; theology
produced society. This is not to say that there was not the
same kind of lip service paid to ideals which modern politicians pay. As the modern politician is always a friend of the

poor because he has to be to get their votes, so Hammurabi could say that the gods established him as king to make justice prevail in the land, to destroy the wicked and the evil, and to prevent the strong from oppressing the weak. Actually Hammurabi presided over a government of the landowning aristocracy; it may have been better than the Canaanite city-states but it was certainly not a government of the weak and the poor.

The Canaanite theology declared that the central benefit which the gods conferred upon mankind was fertility. It was this benefit from which all blessings flowed. I may be stretching a point here to say that this blessing fell first of all upon the landlord and was dispensed through him to the tenants. Fertility is the blessing upon land and upon livestock, and these are certainly fertile first of all for their owner. The gods of fertility preserve a social order which protects and fosters fertility. A stable society, meaning a society of well-defined stable classes, protects fertility. Workers are always available. Wealth is concentrated in a few hands in which it can be fertile and not dissipated in a crowd. Law and legal process safeguard fertility, which means—I fear I become obvious— the means of production.

When the Canaanite society, polity and religion are described in these terms, one recognizes a totally secular state which has subordinated religion to its secular purposes. When Israelite religion proclaimed a god who dispensed not fertility but righteousness as the central blessing from which all other blessings flow, it is evident that there was a deep and irreconcilable difference between the Israelite and the Canaanite worlds. And that is one of the reasons why I have to credit the union of two irreconcilable worlds to David and Solomon, who gave the Israelites what they wanted—a king like all the nations. They and their successors also gave the Israelites what they wanted—a god like all the nations. When they created an Israelite landowning aristocracy, it was evident that such a class could not worship Yahweh. They needed a patron of fertility.

The prophets and the historians tell us that the kings patronized the cult of foreign gods; they use the title Baal, now recognized as the dying and rising god of fertility of Canaanite myth and cult. It is altogether likely that when the introduction of foreign gods is credited to Solomon and several of the kings of Israel, what happened in the temple of Jerusalem was the transformation of Yahweh, the liberator of the oppressed, into the patron of the oppressors. The transformation was not successful; the prophets themselves are witnesses to its failure. But they are also witnesses to its success; they describe a Canaanite society and polity in which Yahweh was worshipped. It follows, if what I have been saying above is correct, that he could only be worshipped as a patron of fertility, in covenant with a king who was the head of the landowning aristocracy. Yahweh could not be converted into a Canaanite god and that says something about the faith of Israel as it is seen in the prophets. But this was not the faith of those who ruled Israel, and possibly not of most of the people of Israel; and upon them judgment fell.

The considerations which I have presented here make one wonder about the term "salvation history" so often applied in recent years to the history of Israel and its faith. If this term is to be retained, then my title "Save by Destroying" must go with it. I said at the beginning of this chapter that such a title is a loose use of the word "save"; and I find the term "salvation history" equally loose. It must include the salvation of Israel by the destruction of its society, its politics and its religion. In this chapter I have tried to present evidence why all of these three elements of historical Israel were not worth preserving. What God saved by destroying Israel, if I may commit an anthropomorphism no more extreme than the anthropomorphisms of the biblical prophets, was his own integrity—in the biblical phrase, his righteousness. He could not remain himself if he strengthened the hands of the unrighteous.

There are strains of the theme of the destructibility of Israel outside the prophetic books. I do not mean to imply that Exodus 32:1-14 is a report of an actual dialogue between God and Moses; but it certainly is the reflection of an Israelite scribe on the infidelity of Israel when it worshipped gods other than Yahweh. The scribe represents Yahweh as determined to annihilate Israel. He does not need Israel; he can and will make Moses the new Abraham of a new Israel. The thought is echoed in the words of John the Baptist (Matthew 3:9; Luke 3:8) that God can raise up children of Abraham from these stones. The statements of the prophets and of the ancient historian and of John the Baptist all agree that God does not need Israel. If it does not fulfill his mission, he can dispense with it.

The thought should certainly be recalled by those who in New Testament terms are the new Israel, the heirs of its gifts and its promises, The study of salvation through judgment gives no reason to conclude that this feature of "salvation history" is entirely in the past, that what God did once he will not do again. The story shows us what God has done to avoid his identification with the Canaanite Baal. One ought to conclude, if one believes in God, that God cherishes his freedom.

## 12

# LAW AND ORDER

IN the ancient Near East law appears with the beginning of civilization; and for practical purposes we can define civilization as the division and specialization of labor. Civilization appears with the city, and the first function of the city is to be a market. The city cannot be governed by tradition and custom; these serve a stable society, but the city is essentially progressive. It can be governed only by law and by courts. Discoveries of ancient Near Eastern laws reveal that Israelite law—which is biblical law—appeared somewhat late in ancient history. The Israelites needed law only when they became civilized. It can be estimated that the collection of Israelite law which appears in the Bible in the five books of Moses contains elements which range from about 1000 B.C. to about 400 B.C. These are extreme dates.

Recalling Chapter 8 of this book, readers will not be surprised that these dates leave no room for Moses. Moses as the Lawmaker is a figure of pure legend, and this is not disputed by modern scholars. Law was attributed to the great Revealer in order to give it the authority of God, who had revealed it to Moses. In fact comparative studies of ancient Near Eastern law have shown that there was a body of common consuetudinary law diffused through the entire ancient culture of this region, and that most Israelite laws can be shown to be derived from this common law. But the attribution of law to Moses is as early as the book of Deuteronomy, shortly before the dissolution of the kingdom of Judah in 587 B.C.

In this book Moses is presented as the founder of Israel

which he was in older traditions. He appears also as the founder of Israelite institutions. When he delivered Israel from Egypt and led it to the frontier of Canaan, he left it with the divinely revealed code of law. Fidelity to this law was the condition upon which Israel's tenancy of the land which God gave it depended. The earliest deuteronomic writers saw that the Israelite traditions were no longer preserved under the monarchy.

The first edition of the book of Deuteronomy, it seems, was meant to be a selection of Israelite laws which seemed essential to the preservation of Israelite religion and Israelite society. They were not expressed in the traditional legal formulae already well over a thousand years old in the ancient Near East. The formulae were expanded and modified by the insertion of direct commands spoken by God and by exhortations to be faithful to the law, motivated by promises of salvation and threats of judgment. Behind both promises and threats, it seems, was the unnamed threat of the great conquering powers of Mesopotamia, Assyria when the first edition of Deuteronomy was written, Babylon after the fall of Assyria in 609 B.C.

After the disaster which swept away the kingdom of Judah in 597 B.C., very little was preserved of Israelite traditions except what was found in Israelite literature. When, contrary to all expectations, a Judahite settlement was established in Judea under the patronage of Cyrus of Persia in 537 B.C., the diligence of scribes in the Jewish community in Mesopotamia had edited and organized most of this literature. This scribal work was continued in Babylon; Ezra, who reorganized the Jewish community in Jerusalem, did so upon the basis of documents which were called "the law of the Lord."

The date of Ezra is still in dispute among scholars; a later date close to 400 B.C. seems more probable than the earlier date of 457 B.C. long accepted without question. At either date Ezra was sent as royal commissioner empowered to impose "the law of the Lord" produced by Jewish scribes in Mesopotamia upon the Palestinian community with the sanction of the Persian imperial government. We are left with the impression, supported by some postexilic Jewish literature, of something approaching total social, moral and religious disorder in the Jerusalem community before Ezra; and hardly any scholar doubts that Ezra and his law were sent by the imperial government at the request of Jews themselves.

It is much less certain, and most of my colleagues would regard it as a wild guess, that "the law of the Lord" was composed to meet this need. Nevertheless, the historian is suspicious when he reads that official measures were taken to meet a need, that these measures included the imposition of a document with the force of law, and that some unknown writers said equivalently, "we just happen to have the document you need." The ancient scribe worked for the purposes his employers set him; but he was also capable of copying and editing documents just because they were there.

What Ezra brought to Jerusalem was, it seems, substantially the five books of Moses as we have them in our Bible. These do recite the great deeds of God in Israel's past; and surely there must have been some among the scribes who read these books with a degree of cynicism. They also include what materials Israelite tradition contained concerning the pre-Israelite ancestors and the beginnings of the world and of humanity. These we have seen. But what made the five books of Moses so important was that element which gave them their Jewish name: Torah. When this name was given the books, it had come to mean not teaching or revelation, but law. Law, in concrete the Law, was the only form of revelation which the scribes recognized.

And it was a truly massive law which the scribes produced. Later rabbis counted 613 different laws in the Pentateuch, which they further divided into 248 commandments and 365 prohibitions. The narrative portions of the Pentateuch could be used to derive conclusions about the will of God and his purposes for man and the world, as could the other books of the Bible. Jesus himself is quoted as justifying nonobservance of the Sabbath (Matthew 12:1-8; Mark 2:23-28; Luke 6:1-5) from a story of David (I Samuel 21:1-6) and a passage from the Torah (Numbers 28:9-10). Neither of these, by the way, were very powerful rabbinical arguments. The Law outranked all other books, and conduct permitted to priests in the cult was not a model for the laity in profane activities. We shall return to the attitude of Jesus toward the Law. But such uses of the Scripture were no more than recommendations; the Law left no options.

God had judged his people for their infidelity to his Law. In order to avoid a reenactment of that judgment, the scribes were determined to collect all the pieces of Israelite law they could find and assemble them into a single corpus of law, inserted in the history of the events in which the law had been revealed. The continued life of Israel could be assured by obedience to the Law which their ancestors had flouted. The Law was seen as a divinely revealed way of life, a complete set of directions which contained all the rules for living in accordance with the will of God and for avoiding that which he did not wish. The Law, as I said, left no options; it also left no ambiguities. God had revealed everything which he wished to be done, and no Jew could complain that he had failed because he did not know what God wanted.

In fact the Law was not a complete code of conduct. There

are some areas of basic civil law which are not covered in the Law. I was once surprised to learn by accident, in the course of pursuing a few points, that neither the Law nor the entire Old Testament contains a clear moral or legal condemnation of prostitution. But in the theory of the scribes nothing was lacking in the Law; what was not explicit could be reached by scribal interpretation. If the precept to observe the Sabbath was vague, it was no longer vague when the scribes had compiled a list of thirty-nine works which were prohibited on the Sabbath. How was this list reached? If you knew that, you would be a scribe; because you did not know it, the Law demanded scribes to make the will of God perfectly clear. If questions arose which the Law did not answer, the scribe would reach the answer by deduction from the Law and from other passages of Scripture. The answer had the full authority of the Law.

What if the scribes arrived at different answers? The Jew was safe in following any scribal answer. Jesus is quoted as saying that the scribes occupied the chair of Moses (Matthew 23:2). What was important was the security of having an answer from God for every question of conduct. If God gave more than one answer it was a token of his abundance. When Jesus was asked about divorce the question was phrased as a choice between the rigid school of Shamai, who permitted divorce for adultery only, and the liberal school of Hillel, who permitted divorce at the husband's demand. Jesus accepted neither school, but went behind both of them to an early verse of the Torah (Genesis 2:24). Other things being equal, an early verse of the Law carried more weight than a later verse (Matthew 19:2-7; Mark 10:1-12).

It seems very clear that what had originally been proposed as a complete code of conduct divinely revealed and as an absolutely safe guide to a life governed by the will of God became a code of conduct dictated by experts. Jesus is quoted as calling this the tradition of men, which the scribes preserved while abandoning the word of God (Mark 7:8). This is one of the texts which indicate that Jesus did not utter a simple and unqualified Yes to the Law; and such texts are too numerous to permit the hypothesis that the early church transformed his simple unqualified Yes to a simple unqualified No.

The disputes in the Gospels about the Sabbath observance revolve around the principle that the Sabbath observance according to Pharisaic interpretation could be inhumane; implicit is the principle that the revealed will of God never commands inhumanity. The discussion of the Law and its observance in Matthew 5:17-48 revolves around the principle that mere observance of the Law does not restrain the evil in the human heart. Again implicit is the denial that the Law is a complete and safe guide of conduct. The Law did indeed establish a moral floor below which conduct should not dip; and in the Hellenistic-Roman world Jewish morality was remarkable for its rigorous standards.

But the Law also established a ceiling above which moral conduct should not rise. This becomes clear in the invective against the scribes and Pharisees in Matthew 23. As the passage stands it is not an exact quotation of Jesus. The number of such criticisms of rabbinical teaching and observance in the Gospels is again too numerous to permit us to suppose that Jesus and the scribes lived in a relation of perfect harmony of thought and sentiment. The thesis of the invective is that the Law is satisfied with a standard of social conduct which does not discourage envy, hatred, rapacity and cruelty. "Whited sepulchers" has become a classic figure to describe what in modern terms is called that image. The phrase encapsulates what every reader recognizes as a valid social criticism; and it is unfair to think that Jesus limited the criticism to his contemporaries.

A passage found in Matthew 22:34-40 (paralleled in Mark 12:28-34 and Luke 10:25-28) is of special interest because of the rabbinical terms in which the discussion is posed. The questions about the greatest commandment in the Law presupposes the rabbinical distinction of "heavy" and "light" commandments, and one's problem was solved. As a rabbi Jesus had an answer. That the answer was two equally heavy commandments—the love of God above all things and of the neighbor as oneself—initiated the Christian moral revolution. The scribal addition found only in Matthew states that all the other commandments (611 in number) "hang" upon these two. Commentators have found this phrase obscure. But if we are moving in a discussion of "heavy" and "light" commandments, the figure suggests that these two commandments outweigh the other 611. Certainly Paul meant this and stated it more clearly when he wrote that he who loves his neighbor has fulfilled the Law (Romans 13:8). Paul could not have read this in Matthew, for Matthew had not yet been written.

Jesus in the same Matthew is quoted as saying that he did not come to destroy the Law but to fulfill it (Matthew 5:17). To say that two commandments have the weight of all the rest certainly implies a kind of fulfillment, a new direction revealed in the will of God. We shall remark shortly that Paul clearly proclaims the abolition of the Law. We shall have to ask whether the reduction of the weight of the Law to two of its 613 commandments does not move in the direction of abolition. The Law is fulfilled when it is perceived that the revealed will of God is that men should love one another. If this is done, all lesser obligations are fulfilled in the very act. The ceiling which the Law placed above moral conduct is removed. By definition love has no ceiling; if it has, it is not love. A saying of Jesus preserved in John 15:13 makes the ceiling of love the surrender of one's life.

We must now turn to Paul, who I said above clearly proclaims the abolition of the Law. That his position is clear does not mean that it was easily reached. Most of the Epistle to the Romans was devoted to this question. We must remember that Paul was proud of his Judaism, his Pharisaism and his Pharisaic strictness. When he wrote, the word "Pharisee" had acquired none of the unpleasant overtones it has since acquired. He had been trained in the skills of tribal interpretation, which are reflected on every page of his writings. He had not been brought up to doubt that the Law was what I have described above. He could not reject the Law without a deep personal revolution; and while his conversion is recorded as sudden, personal revolutions take more time.

It is difficult to trace this personal revolution, which is some excuse for my attempting to summarize it in such a brief space. Even a lengthy treatment would not remove all the uncertainties. It began, it seems, with Paul's conviction that Christ was the total savior both of Jews and Gentiles. If the Gentiles were totally saved, they could not be more saved if they with their salvation undertook the obligation of the Law. This would not be liberation but the adoption of a new burden. It would mean that Christ had not really saved.

By a certain logic it followed that the Law never had saved; and this was a difficult position for a Jew who had been convinced that the Law was that divinely revealed perfect code of conduct. Paul was led to question the Jewish moral superiority over the idolatrous world. His strictures in Romans 2 are not as severe as those of Jesus in the passage cited above—indeed, they are not as severe as passages from Amos, Hosea, Isaiah, Jeremiah and other prophets mentioned in an earlier essay. But they are critical. Paul seems to be writing to those who would say that Christ can do nothing for us, God loves us because we are faithful to his Law. Hence he goes on to talk himself into the position that the Law fosters sin rather than prevents it.

The argument is basically simple. Paul alludes to the passionate forces which rage within the human heart, needing constant restraint if they are not to drive him whom they inhabit to perdition. These are the forces of Sin and Death which man cannot overcome; Christ has overcome them, and faith makes it possible for man to be victorious over both sin and death. The Law gave directions, but it furnished no strength by which one could observe its directions. Thus it became an impossible burden; and salvation means liberation from this burden. Man need not worry about the Law; he need concern himself only with love. Christ introduced love to the world as the governing moral principle; to return where we were, he who loves his neighbor has done all that the Law demands.

It will seem that I oversimplify; others have said so. I believe that both Jesus and Paul meant to simplify; a code of 613 commandments which cannot be followed without a corps of expert interpreters is not simple. I believe that both Jesus and Paul meant to proclaim a way of life which was within the grasp of an adult of the mental age of twelve years, deprived of education and culture, and not endowed with a corps of experts to manage his or her life. If a corps of experts is Christian freedom, Paul made a most unfortunate choice of words.

To tell one that the primary moral action is love will not provide protection from errors of moral judgment. It is a well-known fact that the corps of experts will not protect one from errors of moral judgment either. If a person believes that the primary moral action is love, he or she has an excellent choice of being protected against errors in moral judgment which arise from hatred. I believe it is quite obvious which type of error the New Testament finds more tolerable. If this is oversimplifying, I plead that Jesus did it first.

Of course it took a very short time for the church to restore that Law which Paul—and I believe Jesus—annulled. The corps of experts which the Law produced in Judiasm appeared in Christianity. But, like the scribes, they had to produce the law which only the experts could interpret. The New Testament simply did not leave enough rules; the experts never accepted the proposition stated above that Jesus proclaimed a way of life in which responsible moral decision was within the reach of an uneducated adult of the mental age of twelve years. One of the problems of the corps of experts is that they soon believe that everyone who is not an expert has the mental age of twelve years.

Moral imperialism is a polite name for the desire to manage the lives of others, the desire about which such vigorous language is used in Matthew 23. To the corps of moral experts we have added in modern times the corps of sociologists and psychologists who, working together, are producing a moral code which dwarfs the Talmud both for sheer magnitude and for attention to detail. When one is exposed to some of this modern Pharisaic learning, one sometimes gets the impression that it is devoted to finding reasons why one need not in this instance love one's neighbor as oneself. A classic compendium of Roman Catholic moral theology, used for generations, contained the principle that charity creates no obligation if it involves taking serious trouble. The author was much less tolerant of passionate embraces between unmarried persons. I am not blaming the author for being a product of the system in which he stoked the engines. But it becomes obvious that only a complex moral system can justify refusal to love your neighbor if it causes you too much trouble.

We find that Jesus and Paul proposed love as a substitute for law. John identified love with God himself. I fear that Christian scribes and Pharisees have substituted law for love. Oddly enough, in the long run it is a more facile and supple morality, more easily bent to "the complexities of modern society" and other such things. It puts back the ceiling which Jesus removed and restores the security which so many people find in doing what someone has told them is the right thing. In the community of cannibals who will take a strong stand against eating people?

CHAPTER

## 13

## WISDOM AND FOLLY

**E**VER since the human race began to be human, we assume, wisdom has been taught the young by their elders. Indeed, teaching of the young by their elders is not specifically human; birds teach their young to fly, lions teach their young to hunt, and antelopes teach their young to run and hide. It is, we think, the teaching of wisdom which is peculiarly human. Yet when we define wisdom, as we shall, as the skill of living a human life, we may wonder whether we are so far advanced beyond our feathered and furry friends which teach their young the skills of survival. After all, how often has human wisdom meant much more than that? In any case, my purpose here is to point out that the wisdom books and wisdom themes of the Bible come from a broad and ancient background.

In older and simpler cultures the young could learn everything they needed to know from their elders. I have spoken of the skills of survival. The young learned what foods were safe and edible, how to hunt, how to fish, how to trap, how to care for domestic animals and how to defend themselves against wild animals, how to till the soil. But besides this there was the skill of adapting oneself to other members of the human community.

In a social structure much more stable than our own this skill, like the skills of survival (or should we make this distinction too sharp?), could be taught by communicating a tradition. What the community demanded and what it gave were constants which did not change from generation to genera-

143

tion. The skills of living in community, like the skills of survival, were incorporated in maxims; these were brief, employing metrical form and balance and word plays. These maxims are the proverbs in which popular folk wisdom has expressed itself, it seems, since man learned to talk. In most human cultures in most of human history folk wisdom has been all that the individual needed.

It was not until man became civilized that specialists in wisdom appeared. There are many definitions of civilization, but the one which best suits my purposes calls civilization the division and specialization of labor. In primitive village cultures each family, alone or in cooperation with other families, produced all it needed. For this reason the elders could communicate to the young all the necessary skills. Civilization means a market in which skilled specialists exchange their specialties; one man makes clothing, another produces food, another builds houses. The market itself produces a new specialist, the merchant, whose contribution to the community is simply the delivery of commodities to those who do not produce them. When the merchant appeared it was evident that his commission exceeded the profits of the producers, who really could not profit from their labors.

Merchandising demanded and very probably created a new skill. Writing and reading, it seems, were not devised to record poetry or religious myths or ritual texts, but to keep accounts. The ancient scribe was a specialist in a recondite art. He seems to have been the first to be educated for a profession in a professional institution, called a school, staffed by proved members of the profession which he was learning.

The scribe was not, however, the only professional who arose with civilization; there were also priests and diviners and sorcerers, professional experts in the world above and beyond; producers of luxuries such as jewelry and furniture and monumental buildings, which simpler cultures could not afford; and warriors, specialists in another luxury which simpler cultures could not afford. The scribe, so to speak, possessed the basic skill upon which the whole civilized system depended. His own sophistication is clearly shown by his knowledge of his own importance.

The preceding paragraphs are not intended as a digression to display some superficial historical and sociological erudition. It is important for my topic that professional scribes and scribal schools were the transmitters and preservers of the popular folk wisdom of the ancient Near East in Egypt, Mesopotamia and Canaan. Why the scribes drilled their pupils in the copying of folk maxims we do not know; it is a fact that elementary education in early America drilled the young in writing by using such material as "Honesty is the best policy" and in memory by the use of such memory gems as "A rolling stone gathers no moss," of which I never got an exegesis until several years after I memorized it.

Perhaps the ancients, like the moderns, thought they should attempt to build character while they taught letters. The biblical book of Proverbs is such a collection of popular folk wisdom. The same book also shows that ancient folk wisdom was no stranger to sophistication. "Like a golden ring in a swine's snout is a woman fair and foolish" is a fragment of masculine chauvinism as fresh as the day it was coined. To be fair, I should add that the book of Proverbs mentions male fools much more often than it mentions female fools.

It is not surprising that scribal literature developed a collection of professional scribal wisdom. Most of the samples of this literature come from ancient Egypt. Like medieval Europe, ancient Egypt presented the clerk as the only profession open to anyone with talent and ambition. The ancient scribe joined great power—his masters could not read—with almost no prestige. It was scribal wisdom to recognize the limits of his station in life, to enjoy his power without flaunting it. By and large, he seems to have done this very well.

Scribal offices were found in the centers of power. These were the temples, royal palaces, and great mercantile establishments. From these centers came the documents which have survived: commercial records and accounts, religious myths and ritual books, directions for divination and magic in terrifying quantities, and political records. These are the materials from which modern scholars write the history of the ancient Near East.

It is clear that wisdom here includes learning, again a specialization. Much of this learning is pseudo-learning to modern man. But the myths were serious efforts to make it possible for man to live in a world which often appears irrational. They were genuine attempts to establish good relations with higher powers. To borrow a phrase from a colleague, they were authentic religions which were false. Magic and divination were, as far as we know, as serious an effort to cope with common problems as modern medicine and psychiatry. The collection of laws perhaps shows the most continuity with its. modern descendants.

It is evident that even in early civilization man had come a long way in specialized skills. Most of these skills were jealously guarded; their possessors had no desire to diffuse the emoluments which their skill brought them. Instead of teaching his son where grass and water could be found, the Mesopotamian citizen taught him skills like the skill of the goldsmith.

The development of Israelite wisdom seems to have followed the pattern described above; but the materials for the history of Israelite wisdom are less abundant than the materials from Egypt and Mesopotamia. Israelite religion added a new element, the belief in Yahweh, which had effects upon Israelite wisdom upon which scholars have not reached agreement. Both Egyptian and Mesopotamian wisdom were quite secular, and I mean areligious—not hostile to religion, but not considering religion a factor in the skills of living.

Because so much of Israelite wisdom was derived from Egypt and Mesopotamia, it would be possible to make a selection of passages which would be as secular as anything found in Mesopotamia. Upon this secular structure was imposed, not without some disharmony, the belief that Yahweh alone is truly wise, that the fear of Yahweh is the beginning of wisdom, and that Yahweh alone gives wisdom. The last item really appears only in the legend of Solomon, the paradigmatic wise man (I Kings 3) and, as I once wrote elsewhere, behind the legendary wisdom of Solomon the reader may discern the historical reality of a pompous ass. The legend illustrates the ancient belief that nothing proves wisdom like success, a belief we have not renounced.

The Israelite wise men shared the prevailing belief that wisdom was learned from teachers. The Hebrew words which we translate "wise" and "wisdom" we should sometimes translate as "clever" or "skillful" when, for example, they are applied to carpenters or goldsmiths. The breadth of the word is best seen when it is applied to the advice given by Jonadab to Absalom on how he may rape his sister Tamar (2 Samuel 13). But the basic wisdom was how to live successfully in the human community. This is the wisdom which the young man in Proverbs is urged to learn from his parents.

The basic wisdom was not taught by professionals. The

young man is a fool by definition, and he can become wise only by learning from his elders. If he does not learn, he becomes the worst of fools, an old fool, of whom Proverbs speaks so often. The wise men divide the world into the wise and the foolish. Once the youth has become an adult, they do not envisage a change from one class to the other.

In the Israelite community we find professional wise men and wise women (2 Samuel 14 and 20) whose role and function are somewhat difficult to define. Some were counselors of kings like Ahitophel, the adviser of David and Absalom, whose counsel was like the counsel of God. How did one acquire the reputation of a proved wise person? A few years ago I presented a paper on wisdom to my colleagues in a learned society. Therein I took a view of wisdom which some found too broad. In reference to scribal wisdom I suggested that the scribes, as conservers of erudition, regarded the knowledge of myth (an understanding of the gods and the world) and of political records (collective experience) as wisdom.

An earlier interpreter, now deceased, suggested that the story of Paradise and the Fall should be classified as wisdom, a view now accepted by many. With reference to popular wisdom, I proposed that the wise person was the person who displayed the ability to say what was recognized as the right thing, which might be a suggestion of a course of action; this meant not only the right thing, but the right thing put in a striking verbal formula. Thus in our examples Ahitophel, Jonadab and the wise woman of Abel suggested a course of action recommended by its formulation as well as its content; the wise women of Tekoa found a way to confound David in his own words. It comes to this: Wisdom was recognized as a gift of language and vindicated by success.

In the same paper I proposed that basic wisdom is the knowledge and understanding of human experience. I referred above to the simplicity and stability of the cultures which cherished wisdom. In such cultures tradition is the only source of wisdom. Ideas and practices which have survived the test of time have all the validation they need. In such societies changes normally take two to three generations to be fulfilled, a span of time which is beyond the range of normal experience. When no change is to be expected, "This is what we have always said" and "This is the way we have always done it" are peremptory arguments. It is only in modern civilization that the feverish pace of change makes the experience of the past suspect as a source of wisdom. In ancient times the young were foolish because they lacked experience; but they could not profit from personal experience unless they had the background of collective experience by which they could interpret personal experience. The sage was one who in addition to mastering the collective wisdom of the past was able to add to it by forming wise sayings of his own.

To Socrates was attributed the theory that virtue is knowledge; if men know what is right they will do it, and when ignorance is banished vice will disappear. The theory is not well supported by experience, although it survives in some contemporary theories of education and penology. The wise men of ancient Israel held a similar theory about wisdom. The wise man would not do wrong, not because it is wrong but because it is foolish. In the world of the wise man called Koheleth (Ecclesiastes), there is no profit in it. Readers of wisdom literature have often found it too utilitarian for their tastes. They were taught that virtue is its own reward, even if they never quite believed it.

The Israelite wise men believed that wisdom alone assured success in all one's enterprises. The wise man married a good wife, reared docile children to wisdom, and prospered in farming or merchandising. Wisdom was the crown jewel in the king's diadem; and the wise men would have agreed with Machiavelli that they could tell the extent of the king's wisdom by fifteen minutes' conversation with his councilors. Wisdom was not only the one sure thing in an uncertain world, it rendered an uncertain world certain. Collective human experience had achieved control over the cosmos. To us this should have a familiar sound.

Here the utilitarian character of wisdom appears without ambiguity. The wise man, who for reasons of prudence was also the virtuous man, could not experience failure and pain. In Israelite belief God was the ultimate cause of all things. Man could not, as he could in Mesopotamia, be the victim of demons or of a dispute between gods. Elementary justice demanded that God treat each man according to his own deserts. There could be no failure or pain in the life of a good man. This theory is proposed in an extreme form by the three friends of Job; some interpreters think the theory is there caricatured. It may be, but the theory seems to be implied in many of the wise sayings in the book of Proverbs.

Let me be pardoned for repeating once more that wisdom presupposed a stable society. It had nothing to say to catastrophe, the turn of events which sweeps away the social structure upon which wisdom reposed. We should not think that the ancient world did not know catastrophe. Scholars can trace two catastrophic breakdowns in ancient Egypt. In each of them wisdom not only fell silent, it lost esteem as a safe guide to life. There are echoes in the Hebrew Bible of a similar loss of esteem for wisdom in the great political catastrophe of the sixth century which destroyed the kingdom of Judah.

It is to be noticed that the revival of wisdom in Judaism identified wisdom with the knowledge and observance of the law of God revealed by Moses. Wisdom still meant an effort to find a sure way to be on God's side in any conceivable turn of events, in spite of the saying of Jeremiah (8:8) that the lying pen of the scribes had turned the law of the Lord into a lie. Neither in wisdom nor in law could the desired assurance be found.

The books of Job and Koheleth (Ecclesiastes), which echo the traditional wisdom in form and in themes, are really to be classified as anti-wisdom or critical wisdom. The book of Job appears to be a critique of God's providence, and I would not wish to say that such a critique is not intended. Job is a book of great subtlety, and one is never quite sure that one has captured the author's meaning. But Job more obviously institutes a critique of the conviction of the wise men that wisdom had achieved that certain understanding and that control of the cosmos and of human destiny which I mentioned above. The God whom Job criticizes, blames, insults, and—some critics say—blasphemes is the God of the wise man. He is not a God in whom Job believes. It never becomes clear what the God is in whom Job ought to believe; but he is not a God who can be captured in the formulae of wise men. A god who can be so captured is a false god by definition.

Job's critique of wisdom is based on the contradiction between traditional wisdom and experience, that very experience which the wise men professed was the only source of wisdom. In their theory about virtue and success they had rejected experience, which tells us that virtue does not always succeed and folly and wickedness do not always fail. The book of Job cannot be dated with any precision, but most modern interpreters think it was written after the great catastrophe of the kingdom of Judah. The author treats of catastrophe as it strikes a single man, and no one can say his case is exaggerated. He may indeed exaggerate the virtue of his hero, but that is not important. Job is a representation of a good man; what happens to him should happen only to the most depraved criminal. Reflection will show that formulae like those of Job's friends are still used by good people for those less fortunate than themselves; and this in turn suggests that the book of Job, like all great literature, does not answer questions but makes the reader ask them.

The book of Koheleth is no more easily assigned a date than the book of Job, but most interpreters now think it is one of the latest books of the Hebrew Bible. If Job criticizes wisdom for having nothing to say to catastrophe, Koheleth criticizes it for having nothing to say to anything. The book exudes an atmosphere of weariness of the world, to borrow a German phrase. Wisdom has failed to give man a purpose in life.

In his second chapter Koheleth puts on the person of Solomon—which he soon abandons—the proverbial wise man who enjoyed all the success which wisdom brings to the wise. He built a luxurious palace, he ate from gold dishes, and he had a harem of a thousand lovelies. Koheleth believes all this was vanity. The life of Solomon was no richer than the life of the meanest peasant, and this is not merely because Solomon was unable to purchase immortality. For Koheleth death is merely the final seal on the futility of human existence. Man is simply incapable of achieving or producing anything of more than passing value. The theory that wisdom assures success and happiness is essentially false. As far as success and happiness are concerned, the wise man is no better off than the fool.

As I have summarized the book it is strong medicine, and not all interpreters would agree with my summary. Like Job, the book is subtle. Koheleth does in several passages match traditional wise sayings with sayings which express the cynicism I have summarized. It seems to me that in leaving the antithesis unrealized he leaves clues about his own thinking. Koheleth is one of the least religious of the biblical books.

I mentioned earlier that ancient wisdom was quite secular in character, and that Job criticized wisdom for attempting to control the cosmos and destiny by reducing them to formulae. It was probably against the wisdom which had degenerated into a sure formula for wealth, success and happiness that Koheleth directed his nihilism. If this is all there is to life, then life is vanity and chasing the wind. I do not mean to imply that Koheleth is suggesting a religious view by indirection. I take him at his word. By using the techniques of wisdom he destroyed wisdom, and he said no more because he had no more to say.

# 14

## WHAT MEAN THESE STONES?

**M**Y title is taken from Joshua 4:21; but it is really derived from Millar Burrows, who published in 1941 an excellent popular survey of Palestinian archaeology through most of the twentieth century up to that date entitled *What Mean These Stones?* Archaeology as a scientific enterprise is hardly older than 1920. The earliest explorers were either trophy hunters for museums or lacking the techniques developed since 1920 for reading the history of a site from the remains of human habitation. Even as a science archaeology is basically a trained exploration of garbage and wastebaskets. Much can be learned from such explorations; it is not for nothing that business and governmental agencies go to the expense of shredding their waste paper.

It is necessary for archaeologists at times to remind themselves of all that cannot be learned from garbage cans and wastebaskets. I would not like to have my own throwaways examined; but I do not believe they would tell the investigators much about what I think, unless they contained fragments of my own writing. An illiterate site lacks the basis of interpreting the minds of the people who lived there. We should add that a literate site tells us only some of the thoughts of the people who lived there who could write. What it tells us permits cautious conclusions about those who lived there who could not write. Whatever one thinks about Chicago—and almost everything has been thought—a description of its culture drawn from what is picked up on the lake front beaches on a summer Monday morning would scarcely be a fair picture. But if that were all we had, we might be tempted to think so.

We can study ancient sites by digging—with hoes, not spades; the archaeologist does not like it when a grinning digger comes up with a handful of fragments. The one-story profile of ancient cities meant that after destruction by man, fire or simple collapse from age the builders did not clear the site, but built on top of the remains. Deep foundations appear first in the Hellenistic period (third century B.C.). Greek builders have sometimes embarrassed modern archaeologists by inverting the original layers of debris. The archaeology of the downtown Chicago of 1871 is in Grant Park. But before Greek cities the ancient cities of the ancient world grew into mounds, created by the gradual accumulation of their own debris. At Jericho the city of 2100 B.C. was 80 feet above the earliest city, 6800 B.C. Such hog-back mounds—a *tell* in Arabic—can be seen by the hundreds in the Near East. How does one select a site for exploration? There are quite sophisticated methods of making an educated guess at the location of a rewarding site, but the honest archaeologist is ready to concede the importance of Dumb Luck.

The twentieth century has been as rich in literary finds as the nineteenth. I mention only the most important collections of texts beginning with Nuzu in Iraq (since 1925), Ugarit in Syria (since 1925), Mari in Syria (since 1935), and Qumran in Jordan (1947). Except for Qumran, the archaeology of what was known for nearly two thousand years as Palestine is embarrassingly illiterate. To this list will soon be added Ebla in Syria.

The excavation of a site called tell Mardikh was begun in 1964 by the Archaeological Mission of the University of

Rome under the direction of Dr. Paolo Matthiae. The epigrapher of the mission is Dr. Giovanni Pettinato. The two scholars kept their discoveries well under wraps, not wishing to experience premature reports which are usually distorted, tending to exaggerate the value and significance of the finds, and exploited by the type of journalist who lives by the sensational. But the grapevine of scholarly gossip is a kind of sensational journalism in its own way. I am not as close to these things as I was ten years ago, and it did not reach my ears until 1974, the year of the discovery of the first batch of archives.

Awareness of a possibly sensational discovery led the Italian archaeologists to issue a press statement (*New York Times*, 8/22/76). They were invited to present their findings at the annual meeting of the Society of Biblical Literature and the American Academy of Religion in St. Louis, at which I was present, and at the annual meeting of the Archaeological Institute of America in New York, reported in the *New York Times* (12/30/76). For this presentation I depend on the article of Doctor Pettinato in *The Biblical Archaeologist* (May, 1976, not printed until October, 1976). Inquiries directed to me as one of the resident gurus (a less well qualified guru in this area than in some others) are responsible for this chapter.

Space does not permit an adequate summary of Doctor Pettinato's article. The reader of the *New York Times* reports is not seriously misinformed. The archives discovered in 1974 numbered 42 tablets. In 1975 two more rooms were uncovered which contained about 16,000 tablets. The tablets meant are clay bricks, varying in size from the palm of the hand to the dimensions of a building brick. The signs were inscribed in the soft clay with the end of a reed. The signs were recognized as Sumerian, a system of writing in which each sign represents a syllable, sometimes a word. It was recognized that the language was not Sumerian but a language previously unknown. To this language Dr. Pettinato has given the name Palaeo-Canaanite (old Canaanite). Since biblical Hebrew is a dialect of Canaanite, interest was at once aroused. The archaeologists have dated the texts by standard methods at 2400-2250 B.C.

How does one read an unknown language? Hardly, one may say. Epigraphers are not the cryptographers who unravel coded messages, nor do they employ cryptography. Cryptographers are deciphering a known language. One recalls the success the United States armed forces enjoyed in the Second World War by using American Indians to transmit and receive messages. Ultimately the unknown language will remain substantially unknown without the discovery of such tablets as the syllabaries found at Ebla. Syllabaries were intended to aid the Eblaite scribe to learn Sumerian. The modern scholar uses them in the opposite direction. His task is eased by the possession of grammatical texts and bilingual vocabularies. Palaeo-Canaanite—or Eblaite, as it will probably be called—will be learned. A colleague tells me that in graduate schools of ancient Near Eastern languages Sumerian is elected by more students now than all other languages together. But it will not be learned quickly.

Dr. Pettinato believes he has learned it well enough to publish such statements as those which follow. Ebla was a large city—260,000 according to one text—which dominated a political and commercial empire reaching as far as Sinai, eastern Asia Minor, and Mesopotamia. Its existence suggests the existence of other comparable cities not yet discovered. Cities not previously mentioned before 2000 B.C. are mentioned at Ebla, including some biblical cities. Pettinato has deciphered the names of six kings, including Ebrum (who has been compared inconclusively to Eber, the eponymous ancestor of "Hebrew" in Genesis 10:21-25).

Pettinato did not include in his *Biblical Archaeologist* article a statement quoted in the *New York Times* that he had
encountered the names of Abraham, Ishmael, Israel, Esau
and Saul hundreds of times, and David a dozen times. Nor
does he use the journalistic statement that Ebla has established the patriarchs and their names as historical realities. It is
such unsupported and far-reaching statements that have led
my friend and colleague George Mendenhall of the University of Michigan to say that unpublished material should be
treated as non-existent. And that is the quotation with which I
am tempted to answer questioners who ask what mean these
stones. Until someone reads the tablets we do not know what
they mean.

Few readers of this book will be interested in what Ebla will
demand in the rewriting of ancient Near Eastern history. The
rewriting will be extensive; but the period from 2400 to 2250
B.C. is not the best documented period of the Bronze Age,
and it is doubtful that the existing historical reconstruction will
be overturned. My readers are more interested in the impact
of Ebla on biblical studies, and precisely on that area of
biblical history which is least known. Readers who have
followed these chapters from the beginning have noticed a
certain caution in dealing with the patriarchal stories, a caution which some of them think should be called skepticism. I
do not believe Pettinato ever said anything that could re-
motely suggest that Ebla had established the patriarchs and
their names as historical realities. I did not hear him say it in
St. Louis. I have been misquoted myself often enough to
know that misquotation is the price of being quoted.

There is, after all, a time factor to be considered. Ebla was
destroyed in war by Naram-Sin of Akkad about 2250 B.C.

Once dead, it stayed dead. It was never rebuilt nor resettled. Signora Matthiae (an archaeologist in her own right) said that when they uncovered the library it looked as if the librarian had locked the door at five o'clock and left on the preceding day. This is my point; the library lay undisturbed and unread for 4200 years. From the destruction of Ebla to the first certain date of Israelite history, the foundation of the monarchy in the early 10th century, there is an interval of 1250 years. This is about the interval which separates us from Ethelbert of Mercia and Caedwalla of Wessex. If there is a connection of any kind between two peoples, two cultures, two languages, over such a vast temporal distance, we are entitled to ask to see the connection, not merely to be assured that it has been proved by occult arts that it is there.

A colleague has established a reputation by associating biblical Hebrew with Ugaritic, sometimes in ways too exotic for other colleagues to follow. There are connections, of course, just as there are connections between my writing and Chaucer's; but it is proved that no one wrote anything in Ugaritic after 1200 B.C. Language is a social phenomenon which does not float in the air like an infection. If you find a language, show me who spoke it where and when. I am satisfied that Eblaite was spoken at Ebla—where else? I want to know who carried it through the 1250 years in which it is alleged that it passed into Hebrew.

Archaeology can be called the single factor which has made modern biblical studies possible. As long as the Bible stood in solitary grandeur it could not be understood. It was easy to believe that it told of a world in which anything could happen, a world which was not governed by the laws of our experience—and presumably a world from which we could learn little or nothing about coping with the world of experience. Archaeology put the Bible in a history and culture which it did not produce, in which its people and events became like those of our experience—at the cost, I must say, of some cherished beliefs. But the Bible began to speak to us, because it was seen to belong to our world. For this, I say, archaeology was more responsible than anything else.

This is quite something else from "proving" the Bible, a claim which used to be made often and with enthusiasm. To say that archaeology proves the Bible is as meaningless as to say that it disproves the Bible. I do not know whether the late Edmund Wilson was a fool; he sounded like one when he said that the Qumran scrolls, which he had not read, had disproved the ancient claims of Christianity. If Ebla proved that the patriarchs were historical in the third millenium, it would add complications to an already complicated problem. The only way, it seems, that archaeology can prove the Bible is to do what I said above—to reveal the world in which the Bible was lived and written.

Yet archaeologists are sometimes their own worst enemies. I expressed above some doubt that Doctor Pettinato had made some statements which the press attributed to him. I must say that it would not be entirely out of character with his speciality if he did. If anyone was "The Archaeologist" of the twentieth century, it was the late William F. Albright of Johns Hopkins. Yet those who knew him were aware that he lived through a constant series of "exciting, sensational, revolutionary" discoveries which made all our textbooks antiquated, and in need of rewriting. The discoveries were never quite what Doctor Albright made them out to be, although there were few who dared to tell him so. Oddly enough I do not remember him saying anything like this about anything he had done; it was his colleagues who were making these revolutionary discoveries—although one could hardly fail to notice that Martin Noth and Rudolf Bultmann were not credited with revolutionary discoveries, but rather with fantastic ideas.

How does one tell a revolutionary discovery from a fantastic idea? Study linguistics, Doctor Albright said. Most of his colleagues have been more receptive to the genius of Noth and Bultmann, who had no superiors in their fields in their generation. Doctor Albright, like all of us, was unable to depart entirely from the categories of thought in which he had matured intellectually. I have to add that I never met anyone who exhibited equal flexibility at an advanced age—except possibly Martin Noth.

Archaeologists do like to feed us unproved and untested hypotheses which without the suitable skills and methods one is unable to criticize, or even to suspend judgment. Study linguistics! No one could work in biblical or Near Eastern studies and fail to read W.F. Albright's fabulous production. Yet if one quoted Albright in Albright's presence, one risked a monitory finger and the remark that obviously you did not see his more recent article in which that opinion was revised or rejected.

I reviewed a rather massive book in which the author referred to some of his own articles in journals as, I believe, "youthful indiscretions." He was offended when I asked how many novel interpretations in the book I was reviewing I might find described by the author in the same terms within a few years. It has been said of a colleague in another field of learning that he has never had an unpublished thought. What I have in mind is a significant number of hypotheses, since abandoned, which were proposed with enough assurance for me to depend on them and use them. I imperiled some long-standing friendships a few years ago at a meeting when I criticized some of my colleagues for not proposing their hypotheses with a suitable degree of uncertainty. But they had studied linguistics.

It must be granted that such mistakes are corrected only by the same type of scholar who makes them. The originality and imagination which produce these blunders must be balanced by the painstaking critical judgment which modifies or rejects them. These qualities are sometimes found in one and the same person, but only in a few are they perfectly blended. That is the story of scholarship. One accepts this as the inevitable struggle from ignorance to wisdom.

Yet I cannot help noticing that most of the men who engage in ancient Near Eastern history, languages and literature, and archaeology are present or former biblical scholars. Without any trouble I can think of three men who were once my students who have achieved or are achieving eminence in Near Eastern studies. They have left the Bible far beyond them. One confessed candidly to me once that he was changing his direction because the Roman See has no officers appointed to supervise ancient Near Eastern studies. These scholars know that the only collection of Near Eastern literature which is read outside of graduate schools is the Bible. I suspect it is a desire to find "relevance" which sometimes drives them to premature conclusions, and for the moment to relax their professional competence.

I realize that trying to make a rule against the speculation of scholars is about as practical as a rule against fornication. Such speculation can be both foolish and creative. The pleasant memories of a scholar's life are relaxing with a group of peers who let revolutionary discoveries and fantastic ideas float through the air. Ideas which survive such encounters have been tested. This does not mean that they have been demonstrated, but that they are apt objects for demonstration. On a more formal level this conversation is conducted at the meetings of scholars and in exchanges in the scholarly journals.

What it comes to is this: The revolutionary discoveries of one generation which survive criticism become the common consent of the next generation. And in history and archaeology, at least, there is no way to hasten this process; I cannot speak for other branches of learning, although at points where they intrude into my life I wonder whether they are not jumping to conclusions. The world of scholarship is always aiming at the large picture, the picture in which all the details are intelligible. The big picture is being composed by countless little pictures, painted by individual scholars none of whom sees the big picture. And some may not believe in the big picture or even be interested in it.

There are narrow-minded specialists in every field of learning. One rather famous and now senior scholar for years has attended only those parts of sessions at learned meetings at which he reads his own papers. Plainly others are there to learn, he to teach. But to return to the big picture. One may observe that while the Sistine Chapel was done by a large number of workers, what is expressed is the vision of one man. Committees do not paint the Sistine Chapel. Can scholarship do any better than any other committee? It cannot, unless enough of those who engage in it are moving toward the big picture which they will not live long enough to see.

I hope this will help to make clear why scholarship proceeds at the speed of a glacier. To watch its progress is something like watching a man paint a house, as some wit said in another connection. And I hope this will explain to our readers why I have no positive response to the discoveries of

Ebla. I can wait until the discoveries have matured. I mean by this that the discoveries must fit into what we know of the ancient Near East and specifically into the Early Bronze Age. It is not a tenable hypothesis that all that is known of the Early Bronze Age is a tissue of errors. We may use the analogy of the jigsaw puzzle. One may have a corner, or a human or animal figure. But once one recognizes that the puzzle represents Gainsborough's *Blue Boy*, the puzzle solves itself. The analogy is overstated for the history of the ancient Near East; but once one recognizes that this is the way it had to be, the puzzle begins to solve itself.

I suppose I have said nothing except that the science of archaeology demands unlimited patience not only in its practitioners but also in its observers. Archaeology also demands a kind of dedication which was expressed to me by the first director with whom I worked, the late O.R. Sellers. We do not approach the site, he said, with the intention of proving anything, but simply of compiling the evidence which the site, explored without prejudice, discloses. If this season, he added, proves that all the conclusions we drew in an exploration twenty-five years earlier were wrong, we shall make a positive contribution to knowledge. And I shall never forget that expedition. We found an inscribed shard which was beyond the competence of any epigrapher then resident in what is now East Jerusalem. By accident I found several years later that it was a very common Latin word.

Is archaeology a science? It must strive for the most rigorous methodology and the most careful critical examination of its evidence. In assembling and interpreting the evidence one must hope for a flash of genius. If hospitals depended on the kind of exact methods used in archaeology, you would not drag me into one if I were at the point of death.

# 15

## JUDGE OF ALL THE EARTH

IN the 18th and 19th chapters of Genesis we find a narrative which is strange and terrible. The sequence begins with the charming story of hospitality extended by Abraham to three strangers. It reaches its climax in the smoke rising above the ruins of Sodom and Gomorrah. The incestuous seduction by which the daughters of Lot preserve their race is almost an anticlimax. Perhaps the greatest of the commentators on Genesis in the last century spoke of the "beauty" *(Schönheit)* of the narrative. This is not the word I would apply to a story which evokes the terror and the pity which Aristotle defined as the essence of the tragic.

Modern interpreters are generally agreed that the story of Abraham's hospitality has been tied to an originally independent story of the destruction of Sodom and Gomorrah. But the compilers of the legends of Abraham so arranged their material that the cloud of the destruction of Sodom hangs over the city and over Lot from the first time the two are mentioned. The dialogue between God and Abraham (18:22-23) was not a part of the older story of Sodom; it is a theological inquiry, to be discussed shortly. The story of the ancestry of Moab and Ammon also may have originally been an independent story.

The Dead Sea region must be one of the most unattractive pieces of real estate on the entire globe. The beautiful blue of the water is deceptive. The Sea, 53 miles long and ten miles wide, is always covered by a haze which permits its width to be visible but not its length. The haze is evaporation, the only way in which water escapes from the Sea. The surface of the Sea lies 1290 feet below sea level; beneath the surface the Sea is 1300 feet deep. The Sea is fed by the Jordan and a few smaller streams. The water is 25% solid, six times the solid content of the ocean; one cannot sink in it. One also needs a thorough bath when one emerges; but it is not available. The area of the Sea is one place of which it can be said truthfully that it never rains. Except for the few months of winter the temperatures are intolerable, unless one finds 120° F and up tolerable.

In spite of the fact that it is desert country, the perpetual evaporation of the Sea makes it uncomfortably humid. The ground, so alkaline as to be a glaring white, will not support vegetation, and without vegetation there are no insects, reptiles or birds. There are no fish in the Sea. The few industrious Israelis who are trying to find some way to exploit a totally impoverished land must bring everything with them. A few flowers spring up when water flows down from the hills of Judea after the winter rains; they die quickly. It is a land of death, and the touch of death is not cold. It does appear to be a land which God has cursed; and that is the story of Sodom.

But nothing happened to Sodom. The rift which trapped the waters of the Jordan in the Dead Sea was there long before historic times. This rift begins at its northern extremity in northern Syria and grows in depth and width as one passes southward. It becomes the Sea of Galilee, the valley of the Jordan, the Dead Sea, and the wide valley (although not so deep) through which one passes to the Gulf of Aqaba. The rift then becomes the Gulf of Aquaba, the Red Sea, and finally the great rift of east Africa. Efforts to find the ruins of Sodom, besides presenting a formidable engineering problem, deserve the same serious consideration which we give to efforts to discover the timbers of Noah's ark. Since the beginning of historic times the climate of the Dead Sea region has been as inhospitable as it is now. If one is looking for a memory of a real event, one must accept the supposition that the story has traveled.

The story of the destruction of Sodom is told with an economy which is admirable as art but vexing as a source of history. What seems to be described resembles a volcanic eruption more than anything else. One may compare Pliny's account of the eruption of Vesuvius, or a recent book *(The Day the World Ended;* the author's name has escaped me) dealing with the eruption of Mont Pelee in Martinique on Ascension Day in 1902. This eruption destroyed the city of Saint-Pierre and 29,900 people in a torrent of red hot lava in three minutes, a disaster far greater than the ancient story-teller imagined for Sodom and Gomorrah, but like it in quickness. In fact Mont Pelee gave at least six weeks' warning before it blew up.

But if a volcanic eruption is described, we shall have to move a volcano as well as a city. There is no evidence of volcanic activity in the Dead Sea region in historic times. Some of my colleagues in recent years, aware of the embarrassing absence of the volcano, have postulated the escape and ignition of subterranean gases. Considering the recent importance of natural gas, I am surprised that this hypothesis has not been experimentally tested. But so far the Dead Sea rewards those who exploit it with only a highly impure grade of salt.

In the world of interpretation and of the history of the ancient Near East one learns to burn no bridges behind one. All of the evidence there is suggests that I should treat the destruction of Sodom as no more historical than the deluge of

Noah. Both are myths  and I remind my readers that myth is
an effort to enable man to live with reality without going up
the wall. Both the myth of the Deluge and the myth of Sodom
deal with the fact that reality is sometimes suddenly, inexplic-
ably and totally destructive of human life on a large scale. If
the Deluge and Sodom are mythical representations of this
aspect of reality, take Saint-Pierre; that was real enough. The
problem is not imaginary.

One may think that a gross misunderstanding is rooted in
something as simple and innocent as the Memorare which
Catholic children were taught in my youth, asking for serene
weather for a picnic, a day in the park, an athletic contest, or
other such harmless activities. The prayer immediately per-
sonalizes the encounter between the weather and me into an
encounter between God and me. If I ask him out of his
goodness to grant me serene weather for my pleasure, out of
what does he act if it rains on my picnic? Not out of kindness,
surely, and therefore out of something else. I ask myself what I
or somebody else did wrong. Some ancient Mesopotamian
poets more cynically said that one cannot depend on the
gods to act in a manner which men would call responsible.
They are accountable to no one and therefore unpredictable.
The simple Memorare for a good day turns out to be a
mythological conception of the weather as a personal response of the Deity. Like all personal responses it should be
motivated, and thus it becomes subject to moral judgment,
established by man's moral standards; shall not the judge of
all the earth act justly?

The child who sees his Memorare answered by a tropical
thunderstorm just as the goodies are spread out on the picnic
table might rationalize that this happens because he slapped
his little sister or said "I will not" to his mother. The most

celebrated thunderstorm in American Catholic history was the thunderstorm which obliterated the last day's ceremonies of the Eucharistic Congress in 1926 at St. Mary of the Lake Seminary near Chicago. The rain drenched all of the thousands present without regard to age, sex, state of life, clerical dignity, episcopal purple and cardinalatial crimson. Some cynical observers said that possibly God was trying to tell the American Catholic church something. This remark is just as mythological as the child's Memorare. When we make nature the scene of a personal encounter between man and the Deity we get into deep theological trouble.

The mythological view of nature lies deep in the human consciousness. Just about all over the world the thunderstorm is the manifest presence of deity, both threatening and benevolent. The thunder is the voice of God; the lightning is his bolt, his arrow, his hammer. The earthquake is the reverberation of his giant tread. The sea is a monster which does not devour the land it constantly attacks only because it is restrained by the deity. The volcano is the occasional manifestation of a horrible underworld which is the abode of demons. The ancient Israelites refined the mythology of nature by their belief that nature as the personal response of God was the response of the righteous judge. If this is pursued, it leads to a spurious rationalization of nature which leaves no room for God to act in mysterious and wonderful ways. Israelite mythology of nature, like other mythologies of nature, permitted man to live with some peace of mind on the fringe of catastrophe. Modern men and women have removed the fear by depersonalizing nature; they have not removed catastrophe.

And we have even added some new catastrophes. Why should the destruction of Sodom or Saint-Pierre present a theological problem when the destruction of Tokyo, Hamburg, Dresden, and Hiroshima do not? No doubt because we expect God to be more humane than man is. And to add to the list with a little display of erudition, my sources tell me that it is estimated that in the sack of Magdeburg in 1631 at least 22,000 of the 40,000 inhabitants of the city were killed; this was done manually, not mechanically. This is human, and so we understand it. It is something we could do, or which could be done by people we know or people whom we hire. The Christian conscience of Europe was much more deeply shocked by the earthquake at Lisbon in 1755 which killed 30,000 people (on All Saints Day, yet) than it was by the sack of Magdeburg. This may tell us something about the Christian conscience. War is a civilized activity; earthquakes and volcanic eruptions interfere with civilized activities.

Now let us turn to the dialogue between God and Abraham in Genesis 18:16-33. The dialogue is based on the Israelite belief, presupposed but not argued, that if God punishes by sudden death (and sudden death was always and surely a punishment) then the punishment was inflicted on no one but the deserving. If it falls upon a whole city at once, the Israelite gulped hard and said that they surely deserved it. It is the same dialectic which we can see in the Israelite myth of the Deluge, in contrast to the Mesopotamian myth. Noah and his family were the only righteous people in a totally wicked world, and they had to be saved; or rather the story told that they were saved, so they must have been righteous. The Mesopotamian myth recognized that the anger of the gods can be capricious. Lot and his family were the only righteous people in Sodom, and they had to be saved. The Israelite myth is so formed as to give evidence of the total depravity of Sodom. The myth set the mind at rest, as myths are intended to do.

But myth, like philosophy and theology, sets the mind at rest only as long as sleeping dogs are not awakened. The biblical writer who awakened the sleeping dogs was the author of Job. The presupposition both of the myth of Sodom and the myth of the Deluge was the wisdom of Job's friends, whose dogma was that the judge of all the earth must judge righteously by their standards of righteousness. Job argued from his own experience (fictitious, but more in accordance with the facts than the wisdom of his friends) that the innocent are "punished" as often as the guilty, and that we have to refine our idea of punishment.

Abraham argued that the presence of innocent persons in the guilty city should spare the community wholesale punishment. How many innocent persons does it take? By the kind of haggling which imitates the bargaining of the Near Eastern market, Abraham brings God down from fifty to ten. The argument, which is not without subtlety, makes the execution of judgment in each step of the bargaining depend not on the total guilt of Sodom but on the lack of five righteous men. Less than ten, the story implies, means that God will deliver the few righteous from the sentence. It is implied that it is less a failure of justice to let a large number of the guilty go unpunished than to punish even ten innocent.

This is not only a human standard of justice, but a rather crude human standard; one would expect the judge of all the earth to do better than this. But it is superior to the standards of human justice which were applied at Magdeburg, Tokyo, Hamburg, Dresden and Hiroshima. If anyone had asked Roosevelt, Churchill or Truman whether they would have spared any of these cities because of the presence of fifty "good" people ("good" meaning at least as good as the scoundrels who ordered the bombing), one would have been answered that this is a war not only for freedom and civiliza-

tion but for survival; as for ten good people, do not be
ridiculous. And by the same logic by which the Israelites
justified Sodom, we would have been told by these defenders of civilization that all the inhabitants of these cities were
guilty; they were Germans and Japanese, and what more
proof of guilt do you want?

I seem to be arguing, or trying to argue, that the wisdom of
Job's friends is far from archaic, but it is alive and well in
Washington. The myth of the destruction of Sodom is defec-
tive in its presentation of the Deity and of justice because it
presents the Deity as a western statesman of the twentieth
century. It is blasphemy to think of God in those terms, and
the ancient mythographer is excused only because he did not
know what he was doing. But that does not excuse us from
perpetuating the same myth. Job's friends would have had
trouble understanding Saint-Pierre; the death of Jesus as a
redeeming act would have reduced them to silence—or
rather, like so many Christians, they would have pretended
that it did not happen.

The Noah and the Lot of Saint-Pierre were three survivors.
One, by what may truly be called irony, survived because he
was in an underground dungeon awaiting the guillotine on
the following morning. He lived to a ripe old age, supporting
himself by appearing as an exhibit in Barnum's circus. He was
billed—with some exaggeration—as the only survivor of
Saint-Pierre. No one then or now has proposed that God
spared this murderer because he was more righteous than the
29,900 whom God did not spare. Nor has anyone written a
myth, as the Israelite scribe did, to support the view that the
citizens of Saint-Pierre, "both young and old, all the people to
the last man" (Genesis 19:4) were of a wickedness which
deserved a sudden death in a torrent of red hot lava.

So, the rationalization which we apply at Hiroshima does

not apply to Saint-Pierre. We can say of Hiroshima that they deserved it because they were Japanese; and they could have avoided it by doing things our way. These do not apply to the people of Saint-Pierre. They seem to have been smitten by a stroke they did not understand and which they could not have evaded. The lava fell, like the rain from heaven, on the righteous and the unrighteous, and spared the only proven murderer in Saint-Pierre.

But they did understand, and they could have avoided it. Mont Pelee was a failure not of nature but of man. The mountain, as I have observed, gave at least six weeks warning. Subterranean rumblings were heard by the whole town. Earthquakes became more frequent and more violent, and one fissure swallowed up several hundred workers on a plantation. Large clouds of dense black smoke and occasional tongues of flame were visible at the peak of the mountain. A number of people had quietly fled to the other side of Martinique.

A program of evacuation of the city was proposed. It was proposed by the minority political party. As such it was unacceptable to the majority party, apart from the prospective damage to the value of real estate. Shortly before the eruption the government closed the roads by which people could flee, on the plea that flight would excite a panic. They prevented panic, damage to the value of real estate, and the danger of a growing power of the minority party; and the public authorities and their families were all present at the 8:00 solemn high mass in the cathedral on the morning of Ascension Thursday—the mass which was rudely interrupted by a flood of molten lava at 8:03 A.M. You might think of this the next time you read or hear of the squabbles of politicians.

The Israelite scribe also interpreted Sodom as a human

failure. His interpretation of a human failure was so naive that we cannot really use it for an understanding of the human condition. But when he pointed to a human failure he was pointing in the right direction. He did not realize the solidarity of human failure, although he did realize the solidarity of human righteousness. Very few of the people of Saint-Pierre were active participants in the folly of those who governed them. Those in the rear pews died as quickly as the Governor-General and his wife in the first pew. The Israelite scribe would not have called them innocent, and how innocent are we for the acts of inaction of our government? I still feel guilty about Hiroshima; probably because I am still mythological enough in my thinking to fear that God collects outstanding accounts.

But I cannot say this without entangling myself in the trouble mentioned earlier. We simply cannot think of nature as a personal encounter between God and men. Nature is neither benevolent because God loves us nor inclement because he is angry with us. Nature, we have learned, is a thing, and can be dealt with or thought about only as an object. We moderns with modern knowledge and techniques are able to protect ourselves against certain manifestations of nature which the ancients could see as nothing but the wrath of God.

Yet we sometimes forget our limitations. If the winter of January, 1977 had continued into March, we do not know how many millions would have died. Among other things we can predict the weather better than the ancients could, and this was never a real threat. The biblical curse of the prophets was plague, famine and pestilence. We have had success with these which the ancients would have found incredible. Against human failure our success has been negligible. For catastrophes against which we have learned to protect ourselves we have devised others against which we have no protection except our own good will and good sense.

Ever since I read that book about Mont Pelee I have found myself asking how large a component of human failure there has been in great "natural" disasters. I have found it in some. I have not become a student of the Lisbon earthquake mentioned above. A few years ago during a summer I spent in the neighborhood of San Francisco the citizens were somewhat upset by a BBC telecast under the title of "The City That is Waiting to Die." It was a rather clear charge of human failure before the event. The experts seem to have no doubt that the event is certain and not in the remote future. When it happens there will most certainly be orators and writers who will make comparisons between San Francisco and Sodom. These comparisons will be mythology. Others will ask whether one should have built high-rise structures right on top of one of the world's most notable geological faults. People could not evacuate Saint-Pierre because the place presented too large an investment to be abandoned.

Theology has not yet answered the question of the suffering of the innocent except to accept the revelation of Jesus that suffering has a redemptive value. Neither theology nor believers have ever really accepted this lesson. We shall do well if we can understand that the major agent of the suffering of the innocent is the malice of men; and I do not think anyone is free to dismiss the problem without asking himself or herself whether he or she has at least occasionally accepted the suffering of the innocent as the price of progress, either social or personal.

# 16

## ESAU AND JACOB

THE stories of Esau and Jacob are scattered through chapters 25, 27, and 32-33 of the book of Genesis. These stories present a number of interesting topics for discussion and a number of problems which interpreters have not yet solved. It seems wise to preface the discussion with some points previously made in these pages. The first point is that we are reading a narrative compiled from more than one source; lack of unity and sequence is to be expected occasionally. The second point is that these stories were composed and preserved in a cultural and religious atmosphere which is quite different from our own. In this atmosphere the stories had purposes which we cannot discern clearly.

The brothers are twin sons of Isaac and Rebekah. Where rank in age was important, the first twin to emerge from the womb was the first-born; but we shall see below that the rights of the first-born are ambiguous in the story. The twins are hostile to each other; the hostility begins in the womb and endures through their life until the final reconciliation in chapter 33. The twins struggle for priority in the womb; Esau emerges first, but Jacob holds him by the heel. The heel gives occasion to the first of several explanations of the name of Jacob, based on a false etymology.

The theme of the contest over the birthright recurs in the story of the sale of the rights of the first-born by Esau and the deception of Isaac by which Jacob obtained the last blessing of his father. The interpreter is inclined, when he encounters a text of this character, to assume that he has two or three stories which are roughly parallel. But a close analysis of this text leaves him uncertain about the division of the material among different sources; the composition of the text is too complex to be explained by a simple division of the material.

The twins appear in some parts of the text as ancestral heroes. They are not eponymous; Esau is not named Edom, and Jacob is not named Israel until later in the story in an episode which we shall discuss in the next chapter. But the association of the two men with two peoples does not seem to be operative in the formation of the stories; this identity is rather superimposed. For one thing, it was the kingdom of Judah, not the kingdom of Israel, which had a common frontier with Edom and which conquered Edom under David—a conquest which was lost under Solomon. When the elder is said to be the slave of the younger, it must refer to this historical situation. It is true that there are several plays on the word "red" (Hebrew *edom*), the color of the stew ("mess of pottage") for which Esau sold his rights as first-born; are these efforts of an imaginative scribe to strengthen the association which the original story did not contain?

Interpreters have found in the story a presentation of the opposition between the hunter and the nomadic herdsman. There is no evidence of a hunting culture in Palestine during historic times; this must be the most archaic feature of the story, if that is indeed the theme of the conflict. Like the identification of the twins with two peoples, their identification with two cultures comes and goes in the story. Esau comes home from the hunt unsuccessful when he buys the stew with his rights as first-born. Isaac has a taste for game (somewhat strange in a nomadic herdsman), although he cannot distinguish game from goat meat; and Isaac is deceived while Esau is out hunting.

Esau does not appear elsewhere as a hunter, nor did the Edomites live in a hunting culture. In the parental anti-blessing which Esau receives from Isaac he lives by the sword (27:40). This describes not the hunter but the *Habiru*, the professional soldier and bandit; the two professions have often not been distinguished in history. We do not know that the Edomites produced more of these than the Israelites and the Judahites, whose warlords include Gideon, Jephthah, Abimelech, Saul and David. When Esau leads a band of four hundred men (33:1), we seem to have the proper number for a private army of mercenaries and bandits. That is the number lead by David (I Samuel 22:2). Gideon led three hundred (Judges 8:4); the same number is artificially reached in a secondary story of Gideon (Judges 7:6). Abraham, in the one episode in which he appears as a warrior, leads three hundred and eighteen (Genesis 14:14).

In the meeting and reconciliation narrated in Genesis 33, Esau comes off as much more magnanimous than his crafty brother. Even in the reconciliation Jacob shows an obvious reluctance to accept the escort of a bandit chieftain. In the stories of the sale of the birthright and the deception of Isaac, especially the first of these, Esau appears as the great simpleton. This is scarcely an allusion to Edomites. Mahanaim, Penuel and Succoth are too great a distance from Edom; and if Esau the simpleton is the ancestor of the Edomites, he is the ancestor of a people whose wisdom was highly esteemed in several Old Testament allusions. The inconsistencies in Esau's character are among the unsolved problems I mentioned above.

Let us return to the question of the rights of the first-born. If we could date and locate the story of the twins more precisely, we should have a better chance of defining these rights; the privileges of the first-born were not uniformly the same throughout different periods and places in the ancient Near East. In some cultural areas there were no privileges of the first-born. In other areas the first-born succeeded to all the rights and powers of the father except that he did not become the husband of his own mother. Otherwise he inherited all his father's goods, including the harem, and he had the parental powers over his brothers. This type of privilege can be seen in monarchical succession. But among the Assyrians and in the succession of Solomon these privileges did not go to the first-born son but to that son designated by the sovereign as his successor before the sovereign's death.

Between these extremes lies the "double portion" of the first-born mentioned several times in the Old Testament. This is usually understood to be two shares; thus, if there were two sons the estate would be divided into thirds, of which the first-born would get two; three sons would divide four shares, two to the first-born. Some scholars understood this to mean that the first-born would get half the estate. In fact the text says nothing about the ultimate division of Isaac's estate; the most obvious implication of chapter 27 is that Esau received nothing. In a collection of anecdotes one should not look for perfect consistency.

That the first-born received a special blessing is seen in the words addressed to Jacob masquerading as Esau. The blessing or "testament" to each son was an ancient practice attested in the blessing of Jacob (Genesis 49) and still practiced among some modern Jews, I once learned from a Jewish colleague. The blessing of Reuben (Genesis 49:3) expresses the belief that the first-born son, like first fruits, is the best and choicest product of the source; the quality deteriorates in each succeeding son. This document, like the blessing of

Isaac, exhibits the belief that the last words of a father were spoken with mystical power and insight. The belief in the power and enduring reality of the solemnly spoken word meant that such a word could not be withdrawn or annulled. Had Isaac wished, he could have sent a curse to pursue the blessing given in deception. The story does not contain this element; in the final scheme of the stories of the patriarchs it could not.

The moral quality of the story has long vexed readers and commentators. St. Augustine began one treatment of the passage by asserting that the story is not a lie *(mendacium)* but a mystery *(mysterium)*; the Latin word play is too much for me to reproduce in English (not a steal but a deal?). Like so many Christian commentators, Augustine proceeded on the assumption that the bearer of the blessings and the promises could not do anything seriously wrong. Esau did not deserve his privilege—a view supported by 25:34. But if the stories are independent variations on the theme of the birthright, it cannot be said that Jacob only took possession of what was already his right.

And here we return to the final scheme of the compiled stories. In this scheme the son of Isaac is the bearer of the blessing and promises made to Abraham. Modern scholars are satisfied that the genealogical connection between Abraham, Isaac and Jacob (Israel) is artificial; but the compiler intended to present a genealogical chain in which the acts of God are, so to speak, carried. In the material which the compilers used Jacob was the younger son. There were at least two accounts of how the younger son displaced the elder. The promises and the blessing follow him who holds the position of first-born.

That the authors and the compilers express a moral indifference to the conduct of their hero is not obvious. Most of the biblical narrative is objective, lacking in value judgments. We may not demand that the narrators add "and wasn't that an awful thing to do" every time they relate an unsavory episode. In fact they occasionally do add such notes; see 2 Samuel 11:27. The reader is free to add his or her own value judgments; and the modern reader will reverse Augustine and say this was no mystery, it was a lie. We should not too quickly impose our moral value judgments on the ancient scribes, although I believe it is permissible in this case.

If the story of the sale of the birthright and the story of its theft are variations on the same theme, Jacob comes off much better in the story of the sale. Here he is implicitly charged with no more than a sharp deal and taking advantage of the need of his customer. The modern Near Eastern merchant is praised and admired for this, not blamed; and I am sure that this is an ancient tradition. Esau, as we have remarked, is presented as such a colossal fool that he deserves to lose his privileges.

But the story of the deception is a piece of such crass villainy that one almost fails to notice it at the first reading. The villainy is really instigated and planned by Rebekah; but Jacob has no objection except the fear that he will be caught. Israelite law prohibited making sport of the blind (Leviticus 19:14; Deuteronomy 27:18). There is no hint in the story itself that the blessing and the promises are taken from an undeserving heir and given to a more worthy bearer. Jacob does not appear as a more worthy bearer.

These considerations support the understanding that the theme of the promises transmitted from Abraham through Isaac and Jacob to Israel has been superimposed upon the story of the twin brothers. The intrusion into the narrative gave trouble to an earlier commentator than St. Augustine. Esau and Jacob appear among the examples used in Romans 9:6-24. This passage has been used in the construction of theological theories of election and predestination. Fidelity to this passage, theologians thought, demanded that the election and predestination were antecedent to any merits or demerits; the choice between Esau and Jacob was made before they were born and had done anything good or evil (Romans 9:11). Antecedent election logically demands antecedent reprobation; if one is chosen without any reference to any good he has done, another is rejected without any reference to any evil he has done.

Modern Christianity may find it difficult to believe how seriously the disputes about predestination were taken by our ancestors. They may smile when they are told that the Dutch Reformed Church was ready to break up over the dispute whether election and reprobation were infralapsarian or supralapsarian. They may say that it is such things which make it difficult for them to take theology or churches or even religion seriously. One need not agree totally to admit that there is a good point here. So perhaps Paul's thinking is worth retracing.

His thinking certainly takes off from the choice of Jacob and the rejection of Esau. He took the scheme of the compilation as historical; the story deals with the blessing and the promises. The choice of Jacob is not motivated by the worthiness of Jacob. It is to human perception unmotivated; and to Paul this shows the sovereign freedom of God in his decisions. God is not motivated even by what human beings think of as justice. His example is supported by what we find an even more difficult example: the reprobation of Pharaoh. As Paul sees it the obduracy of Pharaoh is induced by God himself. It serves a purpose; and God is accountable to no one either for his purposes or for the ways by which he serves them. One wonders at this point what kind of debate might be instituted between Paul and the author of the book of Job; this author spoke for the antecedently reprobated.

Paul deserves to have his background discussed to see whether he must carry the load of predestination theology which he has had to carry. I satisfied myself some years ago that election and predestination theology is not a problem nor the solution of a problem but a false position of a problem. Human beings can speak of God only in human terms, all of which fail to catch the reality; but some terms fail more egregiously than others. If theologians were planning and disposing man's ultimate destiny, they would no doubt do it through election and predestination; and depending on which theological school were doing the job, election and predestination would be antecedent to merits and demerits or administered according to merits foreseen by divine omniscience. Both schools have run dangerously close not only to heresy but also to blasphemy, and theology has been improved by the disappearance of this pseudo-problem. I feel safer with God than I feel with theologians.

Paul was anxious to affirm the unimpeded sovereignty of God; it seems hard to overstate this case, but Paul succeeded—not as badly as the theologians, but he succeeded. His fundamental problem was justifying to Jesus the admission of Gentiles into the reign of God on equal terms with Jews. Paul, a member of the chosen people, had been reared in the dogma of the chosen people: the election of the Jews and the reprobation of the Gentiles. To deny this dogma would seen to reject the sacred books and the sacred history. Paul could not justify the admission of the Gentiles from the sacred books as he could justify the election of Jews. He does, both here and in the epistle to the Galatians, argue that the chosen people is not a community of carnal descent, a race, but a community of faith. To belong to this community of faith it is essential that one believe that Jesus is Messiah and Lord. This is the fulfillment of the blessing and the promises. In this context of the epistle to the Romans Paul also adduces—from something of a distance, modern interpreters admit—some texts which, without their context, can be taken to predict or prefigure the admission of the Gentiles.

How does Paul meet the objection that God by accepting the Gentiles is false to his promises? Not by saying flatly that God never promised anything to the Jews exclusively; he was trying to win his audience, not to alienate it. I may note that whatever he did, he alienated it. The same objection, interpreters think, was met in the parable of the workers in the vineyard (Matthew 20:1-16). The workers hired first seemed to think that their hiring excluded both the hiring and the wages of anyone else; this seems to be a very solid belief in antecedent election and reprobation. The answer to their claim was a simple denial of its validity; the landlord said, "It's my money." Had he said this is our days of affirmative action and welfare rights he would have been taken to court, and he would have lost the case. But in New Testament times God was represented as at least as independent as a landlord of New Testament times.

Paul says, less bluntly but equivalently, that it is God's mercy and God's grace, and it is not yours to tell him how he shall dispose of it. By referring to the election of Jacob before any actual merits (Paul was not subtle enough to deal with foreseen merits) Paul applies to the admission of the Gentiles the same principle of gratuity by which the election of the

Jews was explained. The Gentiles are elected without deserving it, just as the ancestors were elected without deserving it. If Jews refuse to acknowledge the admission, they are denying to God his sovereignty and his supreme independence. He is not accountable to the Jews for what he does or does not do for the Gentiles.

Within this application of the story of Esau and Jacob to the conditions of the primitive church it is possible that the allusions of Paul to the obduracy of the Pharaoh and other "vessels of wrath" (Romans 9:22) contain a subtle bite. God cannot be committed unconditionally to anyone, if he is truly sovereign; he is committed only to be himself. Paul probably knew that he was implicitly alluding to Jeremiah 18:1-10, a passage which, like Romans 9:6-24, compares the sovereignty of God over man to the control which a potter has of the clay which he works. He may make the clay what he pleases; if the vessel fails in the manufacture, he will crush the clay and make of the material another vessel for another purpose, and the clay has no complaint. Paul did not make this explicit application of the figure of the potter to his point in Romans 9; if he had, he could have made the point that the sovereign independence by which God can elect antecedently to any merits empowers him to reprobate consequently to demerits. It is impossible for me to be certain that Paul consciously made this implication in the language he uses. He was capable of that much subtlety.

But he does not allow himself to conclude on that note. He believed that the election would survive Israel's refusal to believe; "the gifts and the call of God are irrevocable" (Romans 11:29; "given without regret" is more accurate). For this assurance Paul appeals neither to the sacred text, even with rabbinical exegesis, nor to logic, but simply to mystery, to the unsearchable reality of God. One thinks that had he appealed to this earlier, he might have revised his image of the potter, and in particular his treatment of the obduracy of the Pharaoh. Paul's thought here as elsewhere sometimes progresses like a spiral staircase. It also shows Paul's inability to escape entirely from the "chosen people" syndrome.

I have come a long way from the story of the rival twins, but only because Paul by his unexpected use of the story gave rise to an unfortunate theological dispute, in which few if any of my readers have any interest. My readers are, however, heirs of the theology and the misinterpretations with which I have briefly engaged them. The review may appear to be something like the review of one's past illnesses and illnesses in one's family which a physician asks for when you enter a hospital. To ignore the pathology of one's church and religious experience may be as dangerous as refusing to admit past and hereditary illness. Certainly if modern Christians think they and their church are in perfect health they are in trouble.

# JACOB WRESTLING
## Genesis 32:23-32

ONE of the strangest stories in the entire Old Testament is the story of the wrestling of Jacob. It raises a number of problems which are still unsolved; I do not attempt to solve them here, but to alert readers to their presence. The only parallel in the Bible which can be adduced is the attack of God on Moses when Moses returned to Egypt from Midian (Exodus 4:24-26). This is not a highly useful parallel; interpreters confess that they understand the origin and meaning of the Moses story even less well than they do the Jacob story.

In the sequence of the Jacob legends the incident is placed during the return of Jacob to Canaan from Mesopotamia. He leads his wives and children and his extensive flocks and herds; he is in fact represented as a wealthy sheik. He sends a message to his brother Esau and learns that Esau is coming to meet him with four hundred men. We have suggested in the preceding chapter that while Jacob was becoming a wealthy herdsman Esau was becoming a bandit chief. Jacob is terrified at the news and sends princely gifts to meet his brother. When Jacob and his party cross the fords of the river Jabbok, the nocturnal encounter occurs. After the river is passed, Jacob meets his brother Esau and the two are reconciled.

Interpreters have long noticed that the wrestling story has some of the appearance of an intrusion into the story of Jacob's return. The incident is entirely unmotivated. The adversary of Jacob is not identified. The story presents an explanation of a ritual practice of the Israelites which is nowhere else attested. The opinion that the story is superimposed upon the Jacob legends has long been maintained and is the prevailing opinion in contemporary interpretation. It should be added that to take the story as an integral component of the Jacob legends does not aid in answering the questions raised by the story. It is necessary to set forth at least the major questions.

The first question is the identity of the assailant. The adversary is nowhere called Yahweh, nor does any detail of the story suggest this identification. Nor is it formally suggested that the being is divine. The use of the word "god" in 32:30 represents a loose use of a Hebrew word which in both Hebrew and the cognate languages means a divine or, more properly, a superhuman being. Both in early Israelite religion and in other Near Eastern religions the line between divine and human was not as clearly drawn as it is in western Christianity.

The ancient Oriental believed in a countless number of intermediate beings, endowed with power less than the power of the gods but greater than the power of man, able to do good or evil to man according to their disposition. Such intermediate beings appear in some Old Testament books as "messengers" (angels), emissaries of Yahweh to reveal Yahweh's intentions, to save from danger and to punish evildoing. They correspond to the benevolent demons of Mesopotamian religion.

Hosea (12:4-5) uses the word "god" of the episode, and in the next line identifies the "god" as an angel. While the loose use of the word "god" continues to the late eighth century B.C. (the time of Hosea) and even after, the belief of Israelites had taken a much stricter form than we see in what remains of early belief. While this belief could tolerate an unexplained attack of Yahweh like his attacks on Moses (Exodus 4:24-26), it could not tolerate an attack which a man could successfully resist. Therefore it was not Yahweh but one of his messengers who wrestled with Jacob. Obviously the messenger was not sent to kill Jacob; if that had been his mission, he would certainly have accomplished it. Therefore his mission was only to attack; why this happened gave rise to speculations which we shall touch later.

In the dialogue the question of the name is raised explicitly. The adversary demands that Jacob release him—certainly an indication that the wrestling is on equal terms. When Jacob refuses, the adversary asks his name. Jacob gives it; if he had refused it, the change of name from Jacob to Israel could not have been made. By a popular and probably incorrect etymology the name is interpreted, "Let him be strong against El (a divine name)"; the name is interpreted by modern scholars as "Let El protect." In the Priestly narrative (Genesis 35:10), the change of name is made expressly by God with no reference to the wrestling story.

One cannot argue from the Priestly omission of the wrestling story that the author did not know it. To know the name of a god or a demon was to acquire a degree of control; the god or the demon had to respond to the invocation of his name. A similar belief in the meaning of the name is reflected in the desire of Moses and the Israelites to know the name of the god who promised to deliver them from Egypt. If one was going to address a prayer to a deity, one should know by what name to address him. Where many deities were available, one could not otherwise attract his attention

We may have to look for another being behind the "god"

or the "angel" with whom Israelites identified the adversary. Scholars have found a large number of examples in folklore from various parts of the world of nocturnal demons who lose their power at the first light of day. Such a nocturnal demon seems to be described here; he asks for release before daylight approaches. One does not ask why a nocturnal demon attacks at night. That there is someone to be attacked is reason enough. Yet there may be a reason in this story, as we shall see shortly.

Since such demons are not a part of early Israelite folklore, it has been suggested that the Israelites borrowed a story from Canaanite folklore. If they did, it is very likely that the original hero who successfully wrestled with a demon to a standoff was not their hero Jacob. The hero appears as a man of gigantic, indeed preternatural strength. In only one other passage (Genesis 29:10) is such strength attributed to Jacob, he rolls a stone from the mouth of a well which it normally takes several men to move. But this is said casually without any emphasis. Interpreters have remarked that a man who wrestles all night with a demon does not seem to be quite the same as the timid herdsman who is driven into panic by the approach of Esau and his gang. And perhaps originally he was not the same man.

When we raise the possibility of the attachment of another story to Jacob, we must explain why this attachment was made, especially since the story contains elements to which Israelite belief is usually hostile. Interpreters have adduced several reasons. They have not paid a great deal of attention to the geographical location of the story at the fords of Jabbok.

The Jabbok is mentioned several times as a frontier: of the Ammonites (Deuteronomy 2:37; 3:16) and of the Amorite kingdom of Sihon (later Israelite; Judges 11:22; Numbers 21:24; Joshua 12:2). These data do not permit the reconstruction of the map of a frontier which probably shifted several times in the course of centuries. In addition, the course of the Jabbok, which resembles a large sickle, does not help us to define the frontier. But it is not likely that an Israelite scribe of the tenth century knew any more about the history of the frontier than he represents Jephthah as knowing his speech to the Ammonites in the boundary dispute; and it is obvious that while the war of Jephthah was fought with the Ammonites, the speech is concerned with the frontier between Israel and Moab.

If readers find this confusing, be assured that it is confusing. In spite of the confusion, it is clear that the Jabbok was, during most of the historical period of premonarchic and monarchic Israel, a boundry line between the territory of Israel and some other people. It is not equally clear how much of the course of the Jabbok was a boundry line. It is not clear how much the Israelite scribe knew about the historical geography of the Jabbok. Modern scholars are quite assured of the site of fords of the Jabbok and of the identification of the ancient site of Peniel (also written as Penuel). This is enough to establish the possibility that the story was the account of the entrance into the land which later was the historic land of Israel; and at this point Jacob receives the name of Israel.

The site of Peniel is located on the right or north bank of the Jabbok. Presumably the scribe thought of Jacob as passing into the future land of Israel after he had crossed the river from the left to the right bank. The river at the fords runs through a steep and rocky gorge. The crossing with several thousand head of small cattle would have been a long operation, longer than the scribe seems to give time for. In fact

Jacob crosses the river twice from the left bank to the right bank (verses 23-24+32), and a return must be postulated to the left bank in order for Jacob to be alone at night (verse 25). It appears that in the original form of the story Jacob (or the early nameless hero of the story) had to be alone for the nocturnal encounter and the scribe took some trouble to separate him from his company.

The identity of the adversary possibly appears more clearly; it is the demon who defends the frontier against invaders. Such demons were often carved upon boundary stones as threats to transgressors. The demon is unable to prevent Jacob from crossing the frontier and admits him with the blessing, which is the change of his name. It is as Israel that the invader is a threat and as Israel that he is admitted. The legendary person of Jacob-Israel often foreshadows the adventures of the people of Israel.

Should this be the meaning of the story, it is possible that Jacob-Israel is the original hero of the story; but it would still be unconnected with the story of the return of Jacob with his family, flocks and herds into a land where his father is already at home. The more one studies the legends and the folklore of Genesis the more one seems to become entangled in a hopeless snarl which will never be unraveled.

What is uncovered here is the story of the eponymous ancestor fighting his way into the land possessed by his descendants. His fight is not with people but with a demon; passage is granted. Obviously this story of the entrance of Israel into Canaan is unrelated to stories of an entrance of Israel from Egypt under the leadership of Joshua. Since Israel, we are sure, was a conglomerate of a large number of tribal groups (more than the official twelve), there is nothing really startling that some members had legends of their origin which diverged from what became the official account.

Modern scholars are not sure of the original significance of the name Israel. The more general opinion is that it was the name of a people which passed in folklore into the name of an ancestor who was not originally eponymous. But some have suggested that it was originally not a tribal or ethnic name but a geographical name. There is no evidence for the use of this geographical name before the historic "land of Israel". It seems likely that the Jacob-Israel who could be the hero of this demonic wrestling became an ancestral hero before the people called Israel began to worship Yahweh. This is a development of Israelite religion which we cannot date.

The place of the encounter was named Peniel (Penuel), "the face of El." *El* means "god"; we remind the reader again that this word is used much more loosely than we use the word "god." The name must designate a sanctuary, a holy place designated for worship by the manifestation of the present activity of some deity. We are given here a story of how the place became holy. One Hebrew expression for paying a visit to the sanctuary was to go and see the face of the deity; this expression appears in the name Peniel. Interpreters generally believe that the original expression meant to go and see the countenance of the divine image in the sanctuary. In Israelite worship the divine image was abolished, and the phrase was usually rewritten to read "appear before the face of the deity." There is no evidence outside of the name of the place for the existence of any Israelite sanctuary at this site. This is not a serious problem; other sanctuaries are known only by name. But there is reason to ask whether this was not a sanctuary before it became Israelite and attached to itself the Jacob-Israel cult legend.

It may indeed be nitpicking to say that the story of the wrestling does not justify Jacob's claim that he saw the face of "god" (not the word *El* ) and survived. Often in ancient belief it was held that to see the face of deity was to die. The whole point of the story of the wrestling is that the adversary must escape from Jacob's grasp before the light of day makes his countenance visible. This is probably a point at which the scribe failed to combine smoothly features which were originally unconnected. He also made it impossible for us to find the point of juncture. The nocturnal demon who cannot bear daylight is not the divine being whose vision kills.

The obscurities of the story apparently caused difficulty even in early Israel. As we have noticed, the rejection of belief in demons meant that the adversary of Jacob had to be identified with an angel (Hosea 12:5) or by implication with Yahweh himself. This identification is made explicitly nowhere; but the implication is not difficult. In that case, one must ask to what purpose Yahweh (or his messenger) interposed an obstacle to the journey of Jacob which was not serious enough to halt the journey. Obviously if Yahweh had not wanted Jacob to cross the Jabbok, there were means much more effective than engaging in a wrestling match on equal terms.

There is no doubt that Jacob, in contrast with Abraham and Isaac, is not a moral hero. This was discussed in the preceding essay. We need not appeal here to differences in moral standards in different ages and different cultures. Some of the features of Jacob's conduct may have been more tolerable in the Bronze Age, although it is not at all clear that they were, but this is not the point; even in the Bronze Age they were not admirable. In fact Jacob is just barely on this side of being a scoundrel; as an eponymous ancestor of the chosen people he is more than a slight embarrassment. This seems to be quite clearly perceived in Hosea 12:3-5, already mentioned. Hosea says that Jacob shall be punished for his behavior; and he specifies in the behavior the supplanting of his brother in the womb and of contending, although he was only a man, with God. It seems that Hosea had the same version of the Jacob legends which we have.

Hosea seems to imply that even in the eighth century B.C. the story of the wrestling was understood by at least some as a story of divine punishment meted out to Jacob for his mendacity. Actually the only possibly punitive element in the story is the maiming of Jacob. The cultic practice of not eating the sciatic nerve is not attested elsewhere. It need not be; but interpreters would be more assured that it existed outside this story if it were mentioned elsewhere. Permanent injury inflicted in the wrestling of strong, angry men does not demand miraculous powers; but the story implies that the wrestling is done on equal terms at the tolerance of the adversary, who chooses not to use his supernatural powers until Jacob shows superhuman strength. If the adversary is the guardian demon of the boundary, the injury is defensive, not punitive.

One may indeed adduce mythological parallels to the theme of the punishment of men who were so rash as to challenge the gods. But in these myths the challenge is clear; Jacob was suddenly set upon by an unknown being whose intentions appear hostile. Furthermore Jacob, while injured, wins the match in the sense that he achieved his objective, which in the original story may have been no more than endurance until daybreak; or, if the nocturnal demon was a guardian of the boundary, Jacob achieved his objective of crossing the boundary. If he was punished, it was only a lame hip. I mean "only" seriously; in the same Israelite folklore in which Jacob was lamed for wrestling with an angel in a match he did not invite Uzzah was struck dead for innocently supporting the ark by laying upon it his unconsecrated hand (2 Samuel 6:6-7).

The modern interpreter can live with the almost total lack

of religious meaning in the story by postulating a pre-Israelite origin of a story which the Israelite scribes did not digest very well when they swallowed it into the collected stories of the ancestors. Yet even the modern interpreter feels that the Israelite scribes must have found or added some meaning which is not apparent at a casual reading. The most recent commentator on Genesis, the late Gerhard von Rad, here as elsewhere applies a principle which is characteristic of his work, the principle of successive layers of meaning formed by the enrichment of scribal expansion.

The dominant motif of the narrative von Rad sees as the activity of God, who carries the patriarch toward his appointed destiny and reveals himself as acting. But the dominant theme is enriched also by the theme of the blessing granted to one who has finally achieved faith. And there is also the implicit typology of the encounter of Jacob with Yahweh as a type of the spiritual encounter of the people of Israel with Yahweh. Surely this brief summary will illustrate what is meant by successive layers of meaning. It should be obvious that there can be disputes about which layer of meaning is primary.

Other writers have suggested similar interpretations which I think must be judged moralizing. Karl Elliger, for instance saw a contrast between Jacob's dream at Bethel (Genesis 28) and the wrestling. The first meeting with God is a free promise, a "grace"; the second is an attack of God upon the morally unworthy Jacob, but in good Lutheran theology this also is a grace. H. J. Stoebe, also a contemporary writer, defines the story more simply as an assertion of God's sovereignty against man's self-glorification. It is obvious that the moralizing interpretations depend upon the identification of the adversary with Yahweh the God of Israel. I have suggested that this is an imposition of Israelite belief upon a story which originally did not express this belief, they did it by implication; the adversary is not identified with Yahweh or an angel in the text of Genesis.

This is not to deny that the Israelite storytellers moralized. They did so, beginning with the story of the first human couple and their children. We have studied examples in this book. The story of the sin of David in the final form is a moralizing story, all the more successful because it moralizes subtly. The author of the story of Solomon's sins and troubles was less subtle, indeed he may have rearranged the events in order to make his moralizing perfectly clear. If the author of the story of Jacob at the Jabbok moralizes in terms like those set forth by the authors quoted above, he did it more subtly than any other scribe. May I ask whether the modern scribes, like the brilliant and learned men quoted above, have simply choked on a piece of undisguised pre-Israelite mythology. The Israelite scribe, they believe, must have theologized. I think he did, but in this case he did not moralize.

# 18

## OUT OF THE HOUSE
## OF BONDAGE

THE liberation of Israel from Egypt is the exemplary saving act of God on behalf of his people in the Old Testament. No other event is so often cited as a proof of God's power and will to save; no other act is so often alleged as a motive why Israel should appeal to God for help in need. A theology of the character of God and of his way of acting can be erected on the story of the exodus.

In the Christian liturgy the saving act of the exodus is commemorated. In the rite of the Easter Vigil (as formerly in the rites of Holy Saturday) the night before Easter is the night before the new Christian Passover, the night before the resurrection of Jesus from the dead. Several biblical theologians have pointed out that the biblical ideas of God are radicated in history—that is, in the Israelite experience of God and not in philosophical thought.

One of the leading exponents of this view, the late Gerhard von Rad, faced the problems created by the possibility that, if critical historians are correct or even on the right track, the Israelite faith in the experience of God as savior may be radicated in a non-event. I do not think that he or anyone else dealt with these problems with any notable success. Critical history seems to imperil the distinction between the historical character of Israelite religion and the mythological character of other ancient religions. Myth is a historical nonevent; this does not mean that myth cannot establish a foundation for belief. If myth is an apt symbolic expression of reality, then nothing establishes a surer foundation of belief than the apprehension of reality.

I do not expect any medals for raising this question in this book. But it would be dishonest to readers to imply that the exodus narratives raise no serious historical problems; and we cannot wait until the problems are solved to admit their existence. As I noted previously, if the events of the exodus approached the magnitude implied in the exodus stories, they should have left some traces in other ancient records. besides the Bible; Egypt from 1580 B.C. to 1250 B.C. is one of the best documented periods of the ancient Near East. It is true that the Egyptian scribes (like other ancient and modern scribes) had ways of throwing a veil over defeats; but they did not succeed in entirely blotting them out of the record. Against this we have the proved ability of ancient Israelite scribes to transform or even create events. And these things alone say nothing about what we may politely call certain incredible features of the stories. Nor do they say anything about the presentation of a God who is so thoroughly xenophobic and so wantonly cruel that he too approaches the limits of credibility.

An approach of long standing in scholarship is to rationalize the events. The approach is basically the same in all its forms, although it permits variations in details. We rationalize the narrative by supposing that it is an account of natural phenomena proper to Egypt heightened and magnified to the point of the marvelous. It is quite true that the modern traveler in Egypt wonders, if ancient Egypt was anything like modern Egypt, how a plague of flies could have been recognized as such. But the Nile does not turn to blood, nor has it ever been observed to turn to blood. Hail and thunderstorms are not proper to Egypt. Even a day of darkness is not a common experience; and if darkness is to be rationalized to a dust storm, the ancient Israelites were quite familiar with these. And certainly the death of the first-born children of an entire nation is not an Egyptian phenomenon of nature.

A consideration of these attempts to find a historical memory of the plagues does disclose that the narrative was written by people who had never been in Egypt. The stories are not only not the work of contemporaries of the events, they show less information about Egypt than the modern tourist can get by reading the *Blue Guide*—which, to do it justice, does not contain an enormous amount of information. The reason that rationalization has been generally abandoned by modern interpreters is that it does not explain the narratives. We now look for an explanation in the literary form and purpose of the narratives.

For the reasons alleged above we do not think we are meeting here the kind of historical narrative which we believe we meet in the family history of David or the fall of the house of Omri. We are not dealing with myth like the story of Noah and the deluge. We are not dealing with legend like the stories of Abraham, Isaac and Jacob. Many writers have spoken of an Israelite epic. There are really only two model epics in all literature, the Iliad and the Odyssey. The term is used of other literary compositions improperly and in proportion to the degree in which these compositions imitate, consciously or unconsciously, the poems of Homer.

The exodus story can be called an epic only because it can be considered by us, as it was considered by the Israelites, as the story of the "birth of a nation"; the Israelites would have called it the story of the creation of a people. It lacks almost all of the other features of epic poetry—writing in verse, for instance. We seem rather hard put to find a name for the literary form of these stories. Let us state as a thesis what would better come as a conclusion and say that the exodus stories appear to be cultic recitals.

The cultic recital is an old form of literature, and it is also contemporary. In Roman Catholic ritual any festival which celebrates an event or a person contains a brief recital of the story of the event or the person. The old Latin ritual contained more and longer recitals, including the recital of some nonevents (like the apparition of St. Michael and the translation of the holy house of Loreto) and the stories of some nonpersons (like Saints Philomena and George). We give such recitals a classification of their own because they obviously were composed for devotional purposes. History served up cold is rarely devotional.

I think we are well advised to take seriously the suggestion of the late Martin Noth that the story of the plagues of Egypt is a unit. He meant that it could be detached from the context of the narrative; the situation of Moses and the Pharaoh is the same at the end of the plague stories as it was at the beginning. The plagues do not advance the narrative. Noth thought that only the last plague, the death of the first-born, serves a useful literary purpose; and he thinks the oldest form of the story of the deliverance had only the last plague.

What purpose is served by the story of the nine plagues? The text itself in more than one passage indicates the purpose; the plagues are seen simply as a display of God's power to harass the Pharaoh and his subjects. The Pharaoh is the villain of the place; but ancient Israelite folklore was not sympathetic to the lower classes of hostile people. Indeed the story makes God himself responsible for the obstinacy of the

Pharaoh. One does see a childish view of the Deity and his dealings with mankind.

If we separate, with Martin Noth, the tenth plague, we are left with nine plagues if we keep the traditional number; but how many are there? In my own *Dictionary of the Bible* I used an enumeration accepted by a large number of scholars. The ten plagues are said to be compiled from seven plagues in the Yahwist source and five each in the Elohist and the Priestly sources. Martin Noth does not think the Elohist source can be identified in the plague stories. He counts seven plagues (a significant number) in both the Yahwist and the Priestly writer, with a few variations: the plague of the Nile (foul water in J, blood in P), frogs, insects (flies in J, gnats in P), disease (cattle plague in J, boils in P), hails, locusts and darkness. The original redactor of the documents took the variations as distinct plagues and thus arrived at the traditional nine.

I have alluded above to the failed efforts of interpreters to rationalize the plagues into history. The stories express a belief that the God of the Israelites, unlike the gods of the Egyptians, is the lord of nature who disposes of its powers according to his purposes—which in this case, it must be confessed, are viewed as quite narrow. But while I mentioned the gods of the Egyptians, this is not the way in which the Israelite scribes stated their belief in the power of Yahweh their God; the story of the plagues relates a contest not between Yahweh and the gods of the Egyptians but between Yahweh and the magicians of Egypt. The Israelite scribes normally dealt with the gods of the nations as powerless; magic, on the contrary, was a real power which had to be reckoned with.

No special literary training is required to see that the nine plagues follow the same pattern of narrative, with slight variations in detail. There is the threat of the plague uttered by God, the command to Moses, the infliction of the plague, the yielding of the Pharaoh, the removal of the plague, and the refusal of the Pharaoh to liberate Israel. It is the same type of pattern repetition which we all learned at an early age in the stories of the Three Bears and the Three Little Pigs and Little Red Riding Hood and many other pieces of folklore. It is easy to remember, and as long as the pattern is retained, to introduce variations. It is art, if indeed art of the simplest design. But the pattern is imposed by the artist upon events; he does not discover the pattern in the events, because things do not happen in such patterns.

In the childhood stories adduced above, the story reaches its climax when the pattern is broken. The suspense which the pattern creates is relaxed. In the nine plagues, as we have noticed above, the pattern is not broken and the tension is maintained; the Pharaoh is still obstinate and the Israelites are still in Egypt. The tenth plague breaks the pattern and relieves the tension. The tenth plague is not announced to the Pharaoh. The preparation demanded of the Israelites is prolonged by incorporating the ritual of the Passover dinner into the narrative.

I trust I will be pardoned for pointing out that the death of all first-born males of man and beast in Egypt in one night is simply incredible. And I must also be pardoned for pointing out that daughters did not count. In this instance scholars are sure that the story arose from the Passover ritual; and the Passover ritual is clearly not a historical festival, but the offering of the first-born of men and flocks and herds in the spring, the beginning of the year in the ancient calendar. The Passover at an early date had the theme of liberation superadded. There has been discussion whether the human first-born were sacrificed in a primitive rite no longer preserved in record. There are enough allusions to the practice to support the belief that it was once customary, probably only in scattered times and places. Most scholars do not think that it was ever current in Israel; the human first-born were redeemed from the deity by an animal sacrifice. The Passover cultic recital based the ransom of the first-born on the legend that God spared the first-born of Israel when he totally destroyed the first-born of Egypt.

Such a conflation of ritual themes should not be hard to grasp if we imagine the problems which our Christmas customs would present to a historian a few thousand years from now. How could he unite in a single festival of the Infant Jesus, the crib, Santa Claus, the sleigh and the reindeer, the giving of gifts, the Christmas tree, wreaths of holly, the Yule log, plum pudding and egg nog? How could he deal with Dicken's *A Christmas Carol,* if it were preserved, which does not mention the central theme of the Christmas festival? To make a scholarly analysis of this festival would require much more information about the Christmas festival than we have about the Passover festival. I am suggesting that the story of the nine plagues is an addition to the Passover recital something like the extraneous elements of Christmas mentioned above.

The story of the exodus reaches its high point in the passage of the sea. At this point the Israelites have not yet reached their destination, the Promised Land; and many obstacles lay between them and Canaan. But the escape from Egypt is the first major step, and Egypt ceases to be a threat after they have passed the sea. Should any of our readers consult larger and more erudite works on this problem, they will find the writers attending closely to the geography of the exodus. Several of the place names are real; this is not important. The place names in the Iliad are real too, but the events located in real places are unreal. The Myceneans may very well have mustered a large expedition against a pirates' nest at Troy; Homer did not sing of this, but of the face which launched a thousand ships. My colleagues are trying to find out the geography in the minds of the authors of the story of the sea.

What we call the Red Sea is out of the question, if we are dealing with a real event; if the Israelites knew where they were going (which the narrative in some places leaves ambiguous), there was no reason to go to the Red Sea except to have God divide it for them. It is true that the Hebrew words which we have long translated "Red Sea" in later books of the Bible usually mean our Red Sea; this shows how early the identification was. But the words mean "Sea of Reeds"; and since this phrase has been discovered in Egyptian texts of the thirteenth century B.C., designating a body of water in or near the Isthmus of Suez, scholars have located the "Sea of Reeds" of the exodus in this region. It makes a much less impressive crossing than the one DeMille created.

I am satisfied for myself, however, that the writers meant by the "Sea of Reeds" in the story of the crossing just what the phrase means elsewhere: the modern Red Sea. This means that I am not sure about some rationalizations of the crossing. There is no doubt that a crossing by wading through marshes or taking a rather frightening walk across a sand spit in the Mediterranean (as Roman troops commanded by Titus did in 68 A.D.) is more credible; but such rationalizations assume that the scribes described something other than what happened. On the same assumption we may seek an explanation in the literary form and purpose of the narrative, as we did above.

Scholars also are compelled to make the number of Israelites less impressive. Six hundred thousand armed men (male adults) projects to a total population of 2,000,000, about the population of Philadelphia. As noted earlier, if the Israelites had had these numbers, it would have been the Egyptians who fled from Egypt. It has long been noticed that the number 603,000 can be reached by adding the numerical value of the letters of the Hebrew words meaning "all the members of the sons of Israel." One doubts that this is merely coincidental; and it tells us something about the type of composition used in preparing the stories of the exodus.

It can be suggested, but no more than suggested, that the passage of the sea is an echo of the ancient Near Eastern myth of the victory of the creative deity over the monster of the sea. This myth has left numerous traces in the Old Testament; Yahweh is often said to have overcome or to have bound the sea. In Psalm 74:12-17 language is used which can be applied both to the exodus story and to the myth of the combat. The name *Rahab* is applied several times to the monster of the mythical combat, and once to Egypt (Isaiah 30:7). These passages support the suggestion that the crossing of the sea, the climactic act of liberation, is described in mythological language. It is not described in historical language; and we should not think that ancient scribes did not know the difference. I once wrote that the Assyrian scribes knew the difference between recording the conquests of Sennacherib in western Asia and the recital of the descent of Ishtar into the underworld.

The reader may well ask at this point whether there is any history in the exodus narratives; and if the question is put so bluntly, it deserves a blunt answer; no. If you ask us what really happened when the Israelites left Egypt, I must answer that the sources have preserved no account of what happened, and no material from which we can reason to what happened. I could not say that nothing happened. If the Israelites were in Egypt, they very probably could not have fled the country without encountering problems. No memory of these problems was left.

But a few observations must be made. Whoever escaped from Egypt was not the Israelites; there was no people of that name at whatever date one places the "exodus." There could have been no more than a group who were counted by the Israelites as their ancestors. Most of the Israelite ancestors were Canaanite peasants. American scholars have often adduced the example of the *Mayflower*, which carried very few of the ancestors of modern Americans to this continent. Yet the *Mayflower* became a type of the liberation of the oppressed of Europe; and most Americans could say that their ancestors escaped from oppression in Europe, as the sonnet of Mrs. Lazarus inscribed on the base of the Statue of Liberty has so well expressed it. One American poetess (Mrs. Felicia Hemans), who should have known better, described the *Mayflower* as landing on a stern and rock-bound coast. She should have made a trip to Plymouth and looked at the sandy beach where the Pilgrims landed. The Israelite scribes were not the only scribes who had trouble with geography.

It comes to this: Any event which is important enough to a large number of people to be celebrated in poetry, song and festival recitals will be remembered as it is told in song, story and recital. It seems petty, does it not, to point out that the Pilgrims denied to others the religious liberty which they fled from England to secure. And it seems petty to point out that the Israelites who hymned their own liberation from bondage took a thousand years to accept the belief that Yahweh was interested in delivering anyone else from bondage.

# 19

## HOLY WAR

**F**ROM the beginning of history war has often been conducted in a religious atmosphere and for religious purposes. War as a secular activity is comparatively recent; and the religious atmosphere endured through World War II. Some contemporary Christians who find the holiness of war a revolting contradiction in terms may be right, but they should know that most of history is against them. It seems proper to recognize this ancient tradition before we turn our attention to the holy war in ancient Israel and the Old Testament. There is nothing that we know in the ancient world which corresponds to the Israelite holy war.

The holy war appears both in the narratives of the Old Testament and in laws governing it. The laws of war are found in Deuteronomy 20. A man who has recently bought a house in which he has never dwelt or land which he has never harvested or a bride with whom he has never cohabited is excused from military service. A man is also excused for fear. These somewhat unrealistic excuses imply that God, who wins the victory, does not depend on large numbers.

War conducted against a distant people is to be preceded by an invitation to surrender and accept forced labor; if the invitation is refused, all adult males are to be killed and the women and children enslaved. The peoples of Canaan, however, are to be killed totally; even their livestock is to be slaughtered, and no booty is to be taken. More humanity is shown to the fruit trees of a besieged city, which are not to be cut down. Deuteronomy 21:10-14 deals with the marriage of an Israelite to a woman prisoner of war. Deuteronomy 25:17-19 prescribes a special duty of the total extermination of the Amalekites.

Examples of the holy war in the narratives are found in the book of Joshua. The principles of total extermination are applied at Jericho (Joshua 6), Ai (Joshua 7), the cities of southern Canaan (Joshua 10) and of northern Canaan (Joshua 11). Eastern Palestine was dealt with in the same way (Numbers 21). In the expedition against the Midianites virgin girls were spared from death and booty was taken; this is not a purely holy war. In I Samuel 15, Saul is deposed from the monarchy by Samuel because in the war against the Amalekites he spared the king of the Amalekites and took booty.

The extermination of captives and livestock is called in most English Bibles the "ban." The Hebrew word really means to consecrate, to dedicate to the deity. Persons, livestock and other booty (which was destroyed) were consecrated by being removed from human use. Ancient wars were candid acts of banditry and piracy aimed at plunder. The most valuable form of booty was human beings, who were enslaved. Everything else which was not nailed down was carried off; what could not be carried off was burned.

Many historians think that the mass killings which the Assyrians recorded of their own armies were exaggerated; such a policy would have been unsound economically, and the Assyrians were merchants. This does not mean that they did not kill large numbers for the purpose of frightening others who might think of resisting the Assyrian arms. It is thought that the exaggeration of the Assyrian records had the same purpose of inspiring fear. In all fairness to the Assyrians, nothing that is reported of them by themselves or others approaches the "ban" of the Israelite holy war. The ban was a prohibition against the ordinary profits of war; one may think of it as an effort to raise the moral level of war. Killing people and animals is like burning the flesh of the victims offered in sacrifice.

Modern critics think that the laws of war in Deuteronomy are derived from traditions like those in the book of Joshua. They are artificial reconstructions which never existed as practical rules of conduct. The Israelites practiced war as their neighbors did; war was generally a secular activity, with the reservation mentioned above that war has almost always been conducted in a religious atmosphere. But prayers for victory, like Psalm 20, and thanksgiving for victory, like Psalm 21, do not imply the holy war in the precise sense of the term, which I shall treat more fully below.

Modern critics also think that the narratives of the holy war are also quite imaginative. They do not take the book of Joshua as a historical narrative of the Israelite conquest; in fact most critics think the Israelite conquest of Palestine is a nonevent. The narrative is an imaginative reconstruction formed from local memories and filled out with theological reflection. The archaeology of Jericho and Ai does not support the narrative of the conquest of these two cities. Neither does the archaeology of Hazor support the story of the Israelite conquest. The archaeology does not prove that these narratives are imaginative; it shows no more than that any alleged Israelite conquest left no traces at the sites; in fact it suggests that both Jericho and Ai were uninhabited in the Late Bronze Age.

In this instance criticism might seem to offer some small comfort to those who are scandalized by the holy war; it suggests that the episodes which are most appalling never occurred and that the laws existed in a vacuum. But this comfort would be fallacious. Quite clearly, both in the laws and in the narratives, the ban is proposed as a moral ideal. God himself defeats the enemies; the Israelites are no more than executioners. The book of Joshua presents a land of Canaan which has been emptied of its inhabitants, all slaughtered, so that there is no one left to claim the land or to oppose the Israelites' possession of it. This is the way in which the finished narrative thought of God as acting, or the way in which the Israelites thought God should have acted.

In spite of the unreal elements both in the laws and in the narratives, most interpreters believe that there is an element of historical memory in both laws and narratives. As happens elsewhere, the events which lie at the base of this historical memory cannot be reconstructed. The late Gerhard von Rad reconstructed a pattern of holy war behavior which is widely accepted by scholars. The first action was the consultation of the deity. If a favorable oracular response was returned, the war was proclaimed by the blast of trumpets and the war cry assuring that Yahweh granted victory. The response to the proclamation was voluntary. The volunteers were consecrated to the service; the holy war was a cultic act. As previously noted, ritual purity apparently demanded sexual continence and abstinence from the barber.

The leader of the holy war was chosen because he was manifestly seized by the Spirit of Yahweh, which enabled him to perform heroic feats beyond his normal powers and expectations. The numbers of the volunteers, as we have noticed, were unimportant, for Yahweh was the champion who defeated the enemy. His weapons were nature—as in the storm which mired the Canaanite chariots in Judges 5—and psychology; he inspired a mindless terror in the enemy which drove them to flight in panic. Such a terror is mentioned in Genesis 35:5 (not a war context); in I Samuel 14:15, an episode which shows elements of the holy war; Joshua 10:10; I Samuel 5:11 (not a war context); I Samuel 7:10. These last three passages are among those which are doubtfully historical. On my own opinion I would add to these elements that the holy war was fought only to acquire or to defend the land of promise.

We observed that the war of Saul against the Philistines (I Samuel 13-14) has elements of the holy war; and it was clearly fought to defend the land of promise. Saul's war against the Amalekites (I Samuel 15) and Samuel's war against the Philistines (I Samuel 7) have elements of the holy war but both are doubtfully historical. The war of Deborah and Barak (Judges 4:5) has elements of the holy war, as does the doubtfully historical battle of Gideon (Judges 6:33-8:3). There is no sure trace of the holy war after David, although some earlier practices remained; Uriah the Hittite preserved sexual continence during a campaign (2 Samuel 11:6-13). Uriah the Hittite must have been one of David's professional soldiers; for foreign origin suggests this to most interpreters, although his Jahwistic name (-iah) indicates his adoption of Israelite belief.

Outside of such vestigial practices the wars of David and his successors seem to be quite secular, wars of conquest or of defense. The armies of the kings of Israel and Judah were formed around a corps of professional mercenaries; David and Saul themselves were such. In a culture where war was a routine part of daily life the rigorous observance of the ban would have been impolitic, to say the least. The wars of the Maccabees, which were fought in defense of the religion and of the land, were quite rational—insofar as an activity which is essentially irrational and immoral can be called rational.

The holy war is an excellent argument to show the need of an evolutionary understanding of the theology and the morality of the Bible. A simplified understanding of the Bible as the writing of God himself permitted Christians to take the ethics of the holy war as perpetually valid. In the eleventh century began those wars called the Crusades. The causes of the Crusades were many and complex; of them it may be said that the patent motives were neither as strong nor as numerous as the latent motives. The patent motive was the desire to liberate the holy places where the feet of our blessed Lord had trod from the infidel domination of the Moslems. Implicit in this motive was the intention of delivering such a solid aggressive blow to Moslem power that it would not only cease to be a threat but would be open to Christian—that is, European—conquest. This was dressed in the veil of repossession of the land of promise for its rightful owners—again the ancient theme recurs. The rightful owners, of course, are those who have received the right to the land by the donation of God.

Since the Moslems were unbelievers, who themselves had learned the holy war from the Old Testament, they were not entitled to the refinements of war which the Christians showed toward each other, except to the degree to which the Moslem power to retaliate kept the Christians within bounds. Unfortunately these wars gave a name to any war which was fought in a righteous cause—and what war is fought for anything else? A more recent hero wrote about his war as a crusade in Europe. His enemy, like the Moslems in the Crusades, was not entitled to the refinements of civilized war—using the word loosely.

The Crusaders of the Middle Ages are long dead and cannot respond to criticism. The crusaders of 1945 are still alive, and many of them will resent my statement that their crusade was a phony holy war. I have no intention of making a moral comparison. Since Constantine all wars fought by Christians are holy wars. If the crusaders of 1945 know what the Crusades were, they are welcome to the title of crusade for their effort. Henry Morgan thought he was conducting a crusade against the Popish tyranny of the king of Spain; the Spaniards called it piracy, which it did look like. Oliver Cromwell thought he conducted a crusade against royalists and the Irish. All the religious wars of the sixteenth and seventeenth centuries were crusades; someone has said that the higher the motives of those who fight wars, the more inhumane the war becomes. And not to let the Spaniards off too easily, they thought they were conducting a crusade against the Dutch and the Huguenots.

The holy war is not the only evaluation of war in the Old Testament. Most of the Israelite prophets said something about the wars of Israel and Judah in the eighth and seventh centuries. Let it be established that these were wars of defense against aggression. The aggressive power was Assyria or its political heir, Babylon. All that we know of these two military powers permits us to say that if military resistance was ever justified against anybody, it was justified against Assyria and Babylonia. Yet we read Amos, Hosea, Isaiah, Micah and Jeremiah saying that the military resistance against Assyria and Babylon is morally wrong, it is offensive to Yahweh. They invert the holy war; Yahweh fights with Assyria and Babylon, and their victory over Israel and Judah is assured. There is nothing irrational or inconsistent about their position; Israel and Judah are morally so corrupt that God cannot be on their side. Assyria and Babylon are the rod of his wrath, through which he punishes sin.

I do not know why Christians, who have so often appealed to the holy war as a principle of conduct in modern situations, never appeal to the Israelite prophets as establishing principles of political decisions. Napoleon was wiser, if cynical, when he said that God is on the side of the big battalions. Abraham Lincoln was wiser and not cynical when he told the minister who prayed that God would be on "our side" to pray that "we" might be on God's side. To say that a people or a nation is of a moral quality such that it deserves not God's assistance but his punishment would make us ask what people or nation could be excluded from this judgment.

This leads us back to a remark made above (stolen from the late John Courtney Murray) that war is essentially irrational and immoral. Now let me return for the last time to the crusade in Europe. It was in fact a conflict between two—or shall we say three—demonic powers. You may find one devil preferable to another, but when the deal is over you still have a devil. Jesus once told one of his little stories (or jokes, my colleague Dominic Crossan calls them) about a man who had one devil driven out of his house only to have the devil return with seven friends.

I spoke above of the need for an evolutionary understanding of biblical theology and morality. If anything seems to stand at opposite poles, it is the ethic of the holy war and the teaching of Jesus on nonviolence. I speak of "teaching" with some diffidence; what Jesus said really cannot be condensed or synthesized into a set of rules. If his sayings are turned into rules, the rules contradict each other. They rather communicate an ethos, a spirit, which treats each situation as unique, yet itself remains the same. I realize this is vague and unsatisfactory; yet one has only to deal with a government bureaucratic office to realize how rules without ethos or spirit can drive one up the wall. The sayings of Jesus are not this. When I am urged that Jesus did accept violence when he drove the money changers out of the temple with whips of cords, I go along with the effort to make rules; I point out that Jesus would have encouraged the sending of an American expeditionary force to Viet Nam, if the force had been armed with whips of cords.

Outside of this episode, in which the violence is symbolic rather than real, Jesus neither accomplished anything through violence nor recommended that violence be used for any objective, however noble, as his words and action have come down to us. Recent efforts to identify him with "freedom fighters" would be ridiculous, did they not approach so nearly to blasphemy. It seems safe to say that if Jesus taught anything, he taught men how to die, not how to kill. I am thinking about his saying that they who take the sword shall perish by the sword; I am not even sure that he said it, and I am even less sure that if he said it, it was original. It has a certain "memory gem" quality about it which reminds one of proverbs. And it does not say that drawing the sword is wrong; it says only that drawing the sword carries high risks. The sayings of Jesus communicate an ethos, as I said; and in this ethos there is no room for war, holy or secular.

Christians have lived with this ethos for nearly two thousand years, and they have found ample room for crusades and wars. It is years since I read the way St. Augustine agonized over invoking the Roman legions against the Donatists; with hesitation he did invoke them. It must be understood that the Donatists were quite unsavory—

something like the Hare Krishnas with shotguns. If Augustine could have foreseen the applications of his principle he would have decided that it was better to risk the Donatists. He thought, I am sure, that the "rules" which he found in the teaching of Jesus did not cover the Donatists, and they did not; let me repeat that Jesus communicated an ethos or a spirit which itself remained the same while treating each situation as unique. How could Augustine and so many wise and holy men have failed to see that their invocation of violence turned Jesus into a Zealot, a freedom fighter? The Romans called them bandits, and they often looked like it. When the church opted for the Crusaders, it gave up its missionary mandate.

St. Augustine and the others thought as they did because they found in the New Testament no politics and no public ethics. Jesus addressed his words as we have them to the individual person; he recognized no other area of decision. In the world in which Jesus lived the individual person had no public responsibility; even the Roman government allowed no responsibility to its subjects in the provinces, and no more to those whom it recognized as Roman citizens. Christians in more modern political states, which at least pretend to diffuse public responsibility, have felt compelled to create that political ethic which they do not find in the New Testament.

They have created it, and in so doing they have found the personal ethos of Jesus of no use. They see in this ethos a purely private code—a set of rules which govern one's decisions in the purely private and personal areas of one's life. The areas which are not purely private and personal include most of the concerns and responsibilities of modern man and woman, and to those Jesus does not speak. These concerns and responsibilities are governed by the ethos of the political society, or the business and professional society, of the culture. The ethos of these societies is not Christian; it is secular, in no way different from similar societies in the Roman Empire. Decisions which are made in this ethos are made as if Jesus had not died, as if the Incarnation had never happened. One may make Christian decisions in his personal concerns, but not in his political concerns, his business concerns, his professional concerns.

I cannot solve this problem; if the church claims to carry on the mission of Jesus, it might work on these problems for its members, instead of surrendering to the secular ethos. If one believes in Jesus at all, it seems that one believes that he added new dimensions to human existence, and did not merely give rules for one's private and personal life (or for Christian missionaries, as I learn from some colleagues who work in redaction history).

One must believe that Jesus opened up the way to a truly human existence. Possibly he did this when he showed that the personal area of decision is the only genuine area of moral decision; when one accepts the ethos of the political society and the business society and the professional society one is not making decisions, one is having decisions made for one. If one stands against the ethos, one realizes that this is just about what Jesus did. You cannot be a Christian in private and a secularist every place where your life impinges upon the public; or, to steal another phrase, you cannot serve God and Mammon. Christians who think they can serve both support just wars.

## 20

## STRANGE HEROES

**M**OST cultures which preserve the memories of the past have a Heroic Age. The historical value of the stories of the Heroic Age is slight; legends rather than memories of events are preserved. The Heroes are those who defend the tribe, people or nation against threats from stronger and more numerous enemies. Sometimes they lost their lives in the defense. They are stronger and braver than their fellows, often more reckless (or fearless), not so often wiser or more cunning. Cunning was never esteemed as a knightly virtue, nor was prudence in the presence of danger. The Hero hazards his life quite easily, especially if his honor is challenged.

Western literature acquaints its youth with the Heroic Age of western civilization, or it once did. The Heroic Age of Greece was preserved in the epics of Homer and in Greek tragedy, which drew its themes from heroic tales. The Roman Heroic Age was preserved by the historian Livy, whose stories come to English readers in Macaulay's *Lays of Ancient Rome*. The Heroic Age of early medieval Europe was preserved in Thomas Malory's *Morte d'Arthur*, which reached modern readers through Tennyson's *Idylls of the King* and many other imitators. Less familiar to English readers are the stories of Charlemagne and his paladins, as told in the *Song of Roland*. Even America had its Heroic Age, although it is somewhat clouded by history. I have seen an early book about Davy Crockett which, for incredible heroic feats, rivals the *Idylls of the King* and the heroes of Homer and Livy. One wonders how the Texans ever lost the Alamo.

There are a number of common features in the stories of the Heroic Age. The first of these features we may mention is that the historical quality of the stories varies from dim to nonexistent. This is not merely a question of historic names of historic persons. There may have been a king of Scotland named Macbeth or a prince of Denmark named Hamlet, but it is not of these historic persons that Shakespeare wrote. Hamlet and Macbeth are creatures of Shakespeare's imagination. Odysseus may have been a historical king of Ithaca, but Circe, the Sirens and Polyphemus are not historical. The King Arthur of Malory may have a historic name, but Malory's Arthur is a romantic and anachronistic figure. It is not only that the Heroes perform incredible feats with incredible ease, but that they live in a world which never was.

The Heroes also present an ideal which runs through all the Heroic Ages. It is the ideal of the military hero; his virtues are courage to the point of rashness, as we have remarked, aggressiveness, a delicate sense of honor which becomes vindictive. When Achilles dragged the corpse of Hector around the walls of Troy, he avenged the slaying of a friend which was done in fair and open combat; but the arms of Achilles had been dishonored when they were worn by the defeated Patroclus. The medieval ideal of chivalry shown to ladies is a medieval refinement not found everywhere; Agamemnon seized Cassandra, the daughter of a king, as a slave concubine. The military hero is not always a palatable ideal. And he is always a nobleman; the common people are not only inactive in Heroic Tales, they are nearly invisible. But one must confess that when the Hero develops into the modern ideal of the gentleman (if that ideal still survives), he becomes rather pallid. The ideal of the Hero as a muscle-bound oversexed lout with a low IQ never dies in human society. In our world we dress him in athletic uniform and send him to do combat with his peers.

There is a not unimportant difference between the heroic tales of Israel and the heroic tales of other peoples mentioned above. All the other heroic tales arise in a feudal society in which landowners are the military class, and it is from this class that the heroes are drawn. The stories of single combat which occur in the heroic tales from Homer to Malory are told as if there were no other combatants except the heroes. The heroes are members of a chivalry, and this is meant literally; the professional soldiers of the landowning class are those who own horses and bring them to war, either to draw chariots or in later times to be ridden. Such chivalry was known in the Middle and Late Bronze Ages; the Hurrians were a ruling military aristocracy, and a class of chariot warriors drawn from the nobility appears in almost all ancient Near Eastern peoples.

The Israelites before the monarchy had no landowning class nor any other ruling aristocratic class. What they thought of the horse, the symbol of the ruling class, can be seen in Joshua 11:6-9 and 2 Samuel 8:4; they hamstrung the horses captured in war. One can see in the second passage that David saved enough horses for a hundred chariots; under David and Solomon a military aristocracy and its symbols appear in Israel. The heroes of the book of Judges are drawn from the people, although, as we shall see, some of them come from a professional military class. But the real hero of the book of Judges is Yahweh, the God of Israel. Yahweh is called a "warrior" in Exodus 15:3; the word usually means a professional soldier.

The number of judges in the book of Judges is twelve—thirteen names including Deborah, the only heroine, but she and Barak effect a single deliverance. Not all the "judges" are heroes; the five called "minor" judges of whom no heroic deed is reported are simply names with place of residence and years of judgeship. The late Martin Noth proposed that these were interpreters of law in the Israelite tribal confederation, the only officers whose office extended to "all Israel"; and in fact no other officers of all Israel are mentioned. The confusion between heroes and reciters of law is rooted in the ambiguity of the Hebrew word translated "judge"; the judge is first viewed not as an impartial magistrate but as a defender, a vindicator, an avenger. The heroes, seven in number (eight with Deborah), are such avenging judges.

In the preceding chapter on the holy war we noticed that the leader in the holy war was charismatic; in biblical language this means that he was inspired by the spirit of Yahweh to deeds of heroism and to exercise leadership of the Israelites. The book of Judges betrays no standing political or military structure of leadership. The inspiration of the spirit is mentioned in all the heroic stories except Ehud and Deborah-Barak. The omission of the spirit in the story of Deborah and Barak means nothing; Deborah, a prophetic speaker, is the channel through whom Yahweh inspires Barak.

The effect of the spirit is clearly seen in the stories of Samson; in almost every instance in which he exhibits superhuman strength it comes with the inspiration of the spirit. The spirit is not active in his last great feat; here the belief in the spirit has been contaminated with the legend in which his strength was attributed to his unshorn hair—probably a feature of the consecration of the holy warrior. In

Samson this consecration was a lifetime state. The spirit is abundantly present in the stories of Gideon and Samson; angels appear in the call of Gideon and in the conception and birth of Samson.

Let us make a few observations on each of these heroes, understanding that a brief survey does not do more than pass over the surface of the questions. We can dismiss the two judges Othniel and Shamgar rather quickly; the scribes had hardly more than the names of these heroes. The story of Othniel is filled out by adding the formula which is found in each of the stories of the judges: Israel falls into sin (idolatry), Yahweh sends an enemy as a punishment, the Israelites repent and cry for help, Yahweh sends a savior who delivers Israel; the land has rest for x years. Then the cycle is repeated. The arrangement is obviously artificial. For Othniel even the name of the enemy has probably been corrupted. Of Shamgar (scarcely an Israelite name) even less is told. Othniel seems to be included only because without him the tribe of Judah, the royal tribe, would have no hero in the list.

The first of the heroes is Ehud, a man of Benjamin. It takes nothing from his heroic character that his deed is murder, accomplished by mendacity of a distressing character. He obtains a private audience with the Moabite king by pretending to have an oracular message from the deity. In heroic stories one does not attend to such moral considerations; one admires the combination of boldness and cleverness which the hero displays. That Ehud is left-handed aids his cleverness; a careless search for weapons would attend only to his left side, the normal place to bear arms. The tribe of Benjamin is said elsewhere to muster seven hundred left-handed slingers (Judges 20:16); was there something about the tribe of Benjamin? It is quite coincidental that the name Benjamin means "son of the right." The story of the assassination is filled out by an account of a victory which has features of the holy war; this account is almost certainly added to the story of Ehub.

The reader can hardly miss the realistic and earthy character of the story of Ehud. This does not mean that we have a first-hand historical account; it does mean that in the story of Ehud we hear the voice of premonarchic Israel. One can see that the realism is missing in the added story of the holy war; at least most interpreters have thought so. This same popular character can be observed in the other stories of the heroes; in them also certain parts of the narrative show a similar artificiality. One can hardly imagine a point in the mountains of Ephraim from which the horn could be sounded throughout the land of Israel. Nor could the Israelites have found ten thousand Moabites to slay.

The story of Deborah and Barak is of special interest to the scholar for a number of reasons, not all of which would be of interest to our readers. The late W. F. Albright thought that it was the only event in the Bible before David which could be dated fairly closely; he put it near 1125 B.C. by a process which I shall spare my readers; the arguments are less than convincing, but many have accepted them. It is the only heroic story which is preserved in two versions, one in prose (Judges 4) and one in verse (Judges 5). The Song of Deborah is generally regarded by scholars as contemporary with the event; this recommends it as probably the oldest literary composition in the Bible.

One notices also the emphasis on the role of women in what is a war story. Women rarely play a part in biblical war stories. But Deborah is not a warrior; she is a prophet who delivers the oracle of Yahweh to Barak with a mandate to lead the Israelites and a promise of victory. No other woman appears in the Old Testament in this capacity, although Miriam (Exodue 15:20), Huldah (2 Kings 22:15) and the wife of Isaiah (Isaiah 8:3) are called prophetesses. Barak attests his dependence on the presence of Deborah; his lack of manliness deprives him of the supreme glory, the slaying of the commander of the enemy. This glory goes to still another woman, Jael the wife of the Kenite Heber.

The Kenites were a tribe of traveling tinkers who engaged in war with nobody else; they were the armorers of the world of Canaan. Jael killed the enemy general by violating the customs of hospitality. The guest was sacred, and the host should offer his own life in defense of the guest. The host is strangely absent from the story. One sees here, as one can see in the story of Ehud, that when the Israelites fought their enemies there were no rules. We do not know that there were any rules in the warfare of other ancient peoples; probably not, since the Israelite scribes so candidly report such episodes as matters of boasting. When they said that Yahweh delivers our enemies into our hands, they believed it.

A further emphasis on the role of women appears in the conclusion of the song. The poet does the battle in four verses (19-22); three verses (and more words) are given to the vain waiting of the ladies of Sisera's harem for the return of their lord. I have long wondered whether this interest in women may not suggest the work of a poetess.

Gideon must have been a major figure in Israelite folklore; where the other judges (except Samson) have only one story told about them, Gideon has several. We may include in the Gideon stories the story of his son Abimelek, who was not a hero savior, and we shall not treat him here. I point out only that the story of Abimelek reveals a state of anarchy within Israel. There are two accounts of how Yahweh gave a sign to demonstrate the truth of his promise to deliver Israel through Gideon. In addition Gideon is invited to destroy an idolatrous image in his own city. From this deed he gets a change of name; some scholars have thought the story was told originally about another person.

There are two stories of Gideon's military prowess. The reader can see, once it is pointed out, that the story in 8:4-21 is totally different from the story in 7:1—8:3, which is continued in 8:22-28. One is the story of a battle, the other is the story of the execution of a blood feud. The names of the chieftains are different. The first story has elements of the holy war as well as elements of the incredible. The second story (which has lost its beginning) has the earthy realism of popular story. I call such an element the unsuccessful effort of Gideon to initiate his adolescent son into the realities of the blood feud.

The story of the war is not pure fiction, but a magnified version of a military encounter. The story explains how Gideon was hired by the city of Shechem as its military defender; the story of Abimelek permits us to call him a military dictator. In all probability this contract presupposes that Gideon had become a private warlord, like Jephthah in the following story and Saul and David in the books of Samuel. The city of Shechem hired the bandit chief to defend it against other bandit chiefs. The story of Abimelek indicates that part of Gideon's payment was the right to extract tolls from merchant caravans which passed through the territory of Shechem. Since most overland trade in Israel had to pass through Shechem, this was a not inconsiderable revenue. Such tolls were a normal part of the cost of doing business in the ancient world.

Jephthah was a man of humble origin, and the hackneyed

phrase suits him better than most; he was the bastard son of a harlot, and the name of his father, Gilead, is a geographical name. He is explicitly called a bandit chieftain, the same type of warlord which we have just discussed. The line between bandits and mercenary soldiers has never been clear. This resource was the reason for the appeal of the elders of Gilead to Jephthah. Jephthah demanded as his reward the same kind of military dictatorship exercized at Shechem.

Several questions arise in the story of Jephthah; I deal with them perhaps too briefly. The message of Jephthah to the Ammonites is a model of ancient diplomacy, except that it deals with the boundary of Israel and Moab, not the boundary of Israel and Ammon. Some scribe liked the speech, but did not read closely the context into which he inserted it. Jephthah's vow, which resulted in the sacrifice of his daughter, arose from a primitive type of religious belief and practice. Similar stories are found in other heroic tales; Agamemnon's sacrifice of his daughter Iphigenia is often adduced. Both stories show us the hero committing an atrocity which he thought was demanded by the deity; the theme so described is quite common in heroic tales and in the Old Testament. A third question arises concerning the war between the tribes of Ephraim and Gilead. War is always irrational, but this war seems to be particularly hard to explain. Many scholars suspect that the fragment preserves a memory of a dispute much more serious and probably quite rational, if I may use the word.

Now we come to the last and the strangest hero in the list, Samson of the tribe of Dan. He is a child of promise, like Isaac, Samuel, John the Baptist and Jesus. He is consecrated to God by what is called the Nazirite vow, which has some features in common with the consecration of the holy warrior.

Of no other judge is his consecrtion related in such detail; and no other judge needed this element as much.

Samson is a man of extraordinary strength, like the folk heroes Till Eulenspiegel in Germany and Paul Bunyan in America. He is not a military hero; he carries on a private personal war against the Philistines, and he leads no Israelite troops. His feats of strength are sometimes attributed to the impulse of the spirit, at other times to the unshorn hair of the Nazirite vow. The Philistines appear as an invading military aristocracy who reduced the Israelites to helpless servitude; they maintained their domination until David defeated them.

The moral level on which Samson lives is appalling. He joins gigantic strength to the willful irresponsibility of a spoiled adolescent. I have encountered no other hero with the sheer animal quality of Samson. One wonders how this amoral lout ever became a hero in any stories, and one realizes that he is the only hero who had any success against the Philistines. All his troubles with the Philistines arise from his unbridled lust for women. He has no more respect for life than he has for chastity.

One sees the recurring theme that when the Israelites resist their enemies there are no rules. Nor does God their defender play by any rules. It is not without interest that the stories of Samson present him as the clever hero who is not only stronger than the Philistines but who outwits them. Here is the authentic voice of the defeated who take comfort only in romance. In fact the Philistines were culturally far above the Israelites, and this added bitterness to the Philistine domination.

In Samson the question recurs which we mentioned above; the historical quality of heroic tales is always low. This is easy to see in Samson. A palace or temple which could support several thousand people on its roof supported by two central pillars separated by an arm's length never existed. The other feats are credible as highly exaggerated; a strong, determined man is capable of nearly incredible feats when the adrenalin is running. The stories of Samson do illustrate the low historical quality of the heroic tale. They are not stories of a single deed, like the other stories of the judges; they are collections of anecdotes.

A similar if less obvious judgment can be passed on the other heroic tales. There is no reason to doubt the historical reality of the heroes who bore these names. There is no reason to doubt that the Israelites suffered raids and invasions from neighboring peoples; the Late Bronze Age appears as a highly unsettled period throughout the Near East. The survival of Israel shows that it enjoyed some military successes. But the stories of the judges are heroic tales, not chronicles of wars. We can no more construct a history of premonarchic Israel from these heroic tales than we can construct the history of Arthurian England from Malory, although the problem is not entirely the same in both.

The stories of the judges were not, like other heroic tales, translated into a later world, or into a world which never existed. The world in which Samson lives is real, even if his feats of strength are not. Furthermore, the heroic tales are an expression of national and personal ideals of the ruling class. The Hero of the Israelite heroic tales is Yahweh, the God of Israel. It is unfortunate that he has been drafted into military service for Israel. In the Bible we are not always at the same level of religious belief and understanding. It took the Israelites several hundred years to learn that their Hero is not a mercenary dedicated to their defense; that he professes allegiance to no banner; and that it is possible for him to march with the enemies of Israel.

# 21

## GIANT-KILLER

**A**FTER Jesus of Nazareth and Moses, David occupies more space in the Bible than any other person. Even if one reckons space by alleged authorship as well as by narrative and expository reference, David comes off about the same; for the books of Moses, not written by Moses, are to be weighed against the Psalms, not written by David. In fact David, like Moses and Jesus, has become a plaster image. In the art of medieval cathedrals David looks like a cross between St. Louis of France and St. Cecilia at the organ. The insolent youthful David of Michelangelo is, we think, much more faithful to reality. Michelangelo, a contemporary of the Renaissance mercenary soldiers, was in a good position to understand David.

So many questions arise about David that I may be able to do no more than recite them and leave them unanswered. This is unsatisfactory, but it will suggest to the reader that the reality of David which historians think they can discover is somewhat different from the plaster image which began to take form even in the books of the Old Testament. The first question we may raise concerns his name. The great majority of my colleagues seem convinced that David can be explained as a Hebrew name. There are foreign names in the Old Testament, and they can be recognized as such; Schmidt is as American a name as Smith, but it is not an English name. In the United States there are no foreign names. Similar names occur in cognate languages; and David, probably originally something like Dudu, can be explained as meaning "Beloved" (or uncle?).

But David is not a common type of Hebrew name; in fact there is no other name of this type. And if David can be explained as a Hebrew name, the name of his father Jesse cannot be so explained. It may be an Aegean name, which in the context of David's life and geography means a Philistine name. Others besides me have suspected that David's origins were not Israelite or Judahite but Philistine; it is quite well established that Judah at the time of David's birth was under Philistine domination.

There is more than one story of David's early years and youth, and the stories are not in agreement. This is not surprising; many famous men are the subjects of stories of their boyhood and youth when they were not famous and they were little noticed or remembered. But there is no doubt that Saul meets David, for the first time, twice—which is hard to do. In one story David comes to Saul's attention because he is an experienced soldier and a skilled musician (I Samuel 16:17-23). In the other story David draws the attention of Saul when he kills the Philistine hero Goliath with a sling and a stone, although he is a mere boy.

The romantic qualities of the story of the fearless shepherd boy who faces up to the giant warrior have led most scholars to think that this story is more imaginative than historical. Ancient writers have similar marvelous stories about the skill of slingers; one wonders why, if this skill were so expert and so common, ancient battles were always decided by the charge of infantry armed with pikes. As we shall see shortly, there are ample indications that David was a professional soldier; and it is quite likely that he came from a family of mercenaries. The credibility of the story of Goliath is not strengthened by the attribution of the killing of Goliath to one of David's heroes, Elhanan son of Jair of Bethlehem (2 Samuel 21:19). The matter is still further complicated by the listing among David's heroes of Elhanan son of Dodo of Bethlehem (2 Samuel 23:24). Dodo is remarkably similar to David (see Dudu mentioned above). Few scholars now accept the hypothesis that Elhanan was the original name and David a throne name.

Scholars have raised similar questions about the story of the anointing of David as king by Samuel (I Samuel 16:1-13). The story itself discloses its purpose. In early Israelite belief the king was chosen by God; the choice was manifested by the inspiration of the spirit, which impelled the king to show the qualities of leadership. The community acceptance of the choice was signified by the rite of anointing; in the course of time the rite came to signify less the community acceptance and more the conferring of the spirit, as it does in the story of the anointing of David. Here one must recall that these documents were first prepared by the scribes at David's court. The story of the anointing gives David the necessary theological validation of his kingship. He received the spirit through the ritual performed by a recognized man of God; and from the day of the anointing Saul was a usurper whose throne David was entitled to assume when he chose. Like a real gentleman, he refrained from doing so until Saul had been killed, and even then it took seven more years.

Now we return to the identity of David as professional soldier. This identity is clear in I Samuel 22:1-2; David, a fugitive from Saul, assembles a band of 400 men drawn from the destitute, defaulting debtors, and the discontented. In an earlier chapter we noticed that this number matches well the band of Gideon (300). The character of the members of the band matches the character attributed to the band of Abimelech; "shiftless men and ruffians" (Judges 9:4). Such professional soldiers run through much of the history of the ancient Near East in the Late Bronze and Early Iron Ages (1600-900 B.C.); they are mentioned in Egyptian and Mesopotamian sources under the name of Habiru or Apiru, a name which is now commonly identified with the biblical name Hebrew. The name designated not a tribe but a social class, landless, hiring themselves out to kings and chieftains as indentured servants and mercenary soldiers. It would be surprising if such people did not appear in the early books of the Old Testament.

The books of Samuel place the formation of David's band after his flight from the court of Saul. It is more likely that David first joined Saul as the leader of a company of professional warriors. After his quarrel with Saul, David transferred his services to the Philistine ruler at Gath. One should not speak of "allegiance" or "loyalty" of such men. Theirs was the loyalty of the modern professional athlete, which is given to his paymaster. The mercenary had no national or tribal allegiance; the Habiru as a group were loyal only to each other as long as they remained together by contract. I mentioned questions about David's name and ethnic origins. About the professional soldier such questions are irrelevant. David was neither Judahite nor Philistine.

Wherever the mercenary soldier has appeared people have had trouble distinguishing him from a bandit. The mercenary has always joined banditry to his profession. One may see David practicing extortion in I Samuel 25. It is exactly the same operation which in modern cities is called the protection racket. The reader should notice the response of David when Nabal refused to pay for services which he had not asked (I Samuel 25:13, 21-22). Abigail, the wife of Nabal (and soon to become the wife of David) recognized the threat better than her husband. The modern reader feels that he has suddenly been transferred to the pages of *The Godfather*. In a way he has; it is the same culture. But the modern reader never thought of David in those terms. If he does, he may see why modern scholars think that the denial that David raided the towns of Judah (I Samuel 27:8-12) is more whitewash plastered on by the scribes of David. The bandit, as we said, had no loyalty.

David was not the first nor will he be the last to join a career of banditry with a superior degree of political ambition and crown his ambition with overwhelming success. William the Conqueror (who had at least one feature in common with Jephthah) founded on banditry a quite enduring enterprise. Historians have noticed that David's rise from bandit chieftain to King of the dual monarchy of Israel and Judah and then to head of the largest empire of the ancient Near East between the empire of Egypt and the empire of Assyria was achieved with perfect timing. David never took an opportunity until it was ripe, and he never failed to take an opportunity when it was ripe. His two kingdoms of Israel and Judah came to him by the free offer of the elders of those communities; so the story is reported, although the story does not exclude some hidden stimulation of the wills of the elders such as is reported in I Samuel 30:26-30.

Historians have noticed how frequently those who are obstacles to the advancement of David die at the opportune moment: Saul and Jonathan, Abner, Ishbaal. There is no implication that David was responsible for these deaths. For all those mentioned, David mourned publicly and executed the killers. One might include Absalom, except that to be opportune his death would have had to occur earlier. The question one asks is whether the killers did not think they were reading the desires of David. I suppose the inquirer must have become somewhat cynical about David even to ask these questions. The fact is that the more closely one studies David the more difficult it becomes to attribute to him anything but base motives. Most men who have fulfilled as successfully their political ambitions have exhibited base motives. David is in bad company among the political successes of history.

In addition, as we shall see in detail in the chapter which follows, David established the type of monarchy and aristocracy which the Israelite tribal confederation had rejected. The monarchy of the Canaanite city-states was supported by a theology which presented the king as the ruler designated by the gods, the mediator between the gods and the subjects of the king. The scribes of David created a theology which gave David and his royal family the divine authentication which raised him above the level of the warlord. It is difficult to discuss this; many of the elements of this theology have passed into traditional Christian belief, and not all of these elements were worthy of preservation.

To take one example: Christ is a customary designation of Jesus among Christians, and their own name of Christians attests their belief that Jesus has this title as proper. Yet the word *christos* translates the Hebrew word which comes to us in English as Messiah; and this word means the anointed one, the savior hero who is impelled by the spirit to lead his people to victory against their enemies. The anointing of the Israelite king conferred the spirit upon him not as a passing impulse but as a permanent charismatic gift. If one finds difficulty in finding a single line of development from the bloodthirsty oversexed bandit of whom we are writing to Jesus of Nazareth, let him be assured that the difficulty is real.

The basic theological element in the monarchy of David

was the gift of the spirit, proved in fact by success and symbolized in ritual by the anointing. The gift of the spirit, proved by success, needed the authentication of divine revelation. The revelation was uttered by an accepted spokesman of the deity, who in the story of David is Samuel. Samuel is also the spokesman through whom Saul was chosen and rejected. The historian doubts, as I have said, the story of the anointing of David when David was a boy; but there is no reason to doubt that Samuel accepted David as God's new man chosen to replace the failed hero Saul. Certain critical problems arise when the documents were first prepared in the offices of the man whom they authenticate. In any case, David was anointed both as king of Judah (2 Samuel 2:4) and as king of Israel (2 Samuel 5:3); and while the anointing is credited to the elders of Judah and Israel, the actual rite was no doubt performed by men who had a religious role. David ruled a dual monarchy; that is, one king reigned over two kingdoms, Judah and Israel, and they remained distinct throughout the life of David.

These stories of the choice and anointing of David by the elders deal with the political realities of the time. The election of David by Yahweh had to be announced by a prophet, a vehicle of revelation. We have, as noticed, the revelation given by Samuel. More important is the announcement by the prophet Nathan, which occurs in at least three forms in the Bible (2 Samuel 7; I Chronicles 17; Psalm 89:20-38). This oracle declares the divine election not only of David but of his dynasty. One of the problems in all forms of politics has been the transfer of power. In monarchical politics this has often been solved by the extermination of one house in favor of another. The house of David is removed from judgment; the individual member of the dynasty will be punished for his own sins, but the dynasty will never be punished and never dethroned. This oracle, of course, was not verified by history; the dynasty of David fell in 587 B.C., never to be restored. Even if the belief of some Christians that the eternal dynasty promised to David was verified in the spiritual kingship of Jesus, the dethronement of 600 years is scarcely faithful to the oracle of Nathan, which leaves no room even for a temporary dethronement. Furthermore, neither David nor Nathan was thinking of a spiritual kingship.

The theology of the scribes put David and his dynasty into a covenant relationship with Yahweh. The covenant was modeled after the convenant of Yahewh with Israel, but it went further. The covenant of Yahweh with Israel promised no eternal election unconditioned by the fidelity of Israel to covenant obligations, as the covenant of David was unconditioned. Furthermore, in the theology of David's scribes the covenant of Israel was subsumed under the covenant of David; Israel was in covenant with Yahweh not as the people of Yahweh but as the people of David, who was in covenant with Yahweh. If they remained the people of David, they came under the eternal covenant which included no possibility of being voided. It should need no explanation to show that these were serious modifications in the premonarchic idea of covenant. The covenant, instead of depending on the free moral choice of God, was dependent on a political system which declared itself independent of the moral will of God. This may be less a modification of the idea of covenant than a denial of the idea of covenant.

Much of the biblical narrative about David is found in what is called the succession narrative (2 Samuel 9-20 & I Kings 1-2). This narrative is regarded by critics as a single composition written by a single author who was contemporary with events, a member of the court of David. The narrative certainly does explain why Solomon rather than any older son of David became king; it was due to the selection of David himself, as well as to the death of those sons of David who might have succeeded David had they survived. There was no law of primogeniture; nor did succession always follow primogeniture in Near Eastern monarchies. The Assyrian kings designated the crown prince at an age early enough for the prince to be associated with his father in government. David, on the contrary, let matters slide; and most historians think they see a palace intrigue in the story more complex than the narrative describes.

Whether the author intended it or not, he has in the succession story described the sins of the king punished by the nearly total breakdown of his kingdom and his success. The sordid story of the adultery of David and Bathsheba and the murder of Uriah is one of the few deeds of which a biblical narrator passes a moral judgment (2 Samual 11:27). One should not think that such abuse of power was common in ancient Near Eastern monarchies; it has never been common anywhere. It is altogether in keeping with the character of David which I have been establishing in this essay; a man to whom violence is a way of life, consumed by ambition for power and wealth, unrestrained by any moral principle except considerations of prudence and public opinion.

Most readers have found the sons of David—Amnon, Absalom, Adonijah—rather horrible young men. It has occurred to some of the readers that these horrible young men were chips off the old block; it is they, and not the simple shepherd boy, who show us what the young David was. In another chapter I shall try to show that Solomon, who like his father has been encased in plaster, was another chip off the old block and the biggest.

The moral level of the actors and actresses of the story is so obviously low as to need no explanation. The reader may not realize that the story gives occasion to reflect on the alleged political genius and success of David. In these chapters an insurrection is mounted in David's first political success, the kingdom of Judah; and David had to flee his own palace and his own city in haste. There was also an insurrection in the kingdom of Israel. The author has separated this from the Absalom insurrection (2 Samuel 20); but some historians think this division was a matter of convenience, and that both insurrections happened nearly simultaneously.

In any case, the rising, which seems to have been sudden, shows that the leaders spoke to a discontented people. This does not give us the picture of a beloved monarch. David saved his life and his throne only because of the loyalty of his hired professional soldiers; and it is legitimate to suppose that these fared better under the monarchy of David than the peasants of Israel and Judah. The insurrections were suppressed by force; the narrative mentions none of the things normally done to rebellious subjects in ancient Near Eastern kingdoms and empires. I do not believe we wrong David in supposing that he was as normal a ruler in this respect as he was in others, and that he was no more clement to the Israelites and Judahites than he was to the Moabites (2 Samuel 8:2) and the Ammonites (2 Samuel 12:31). Nothing in the literary sources about David suggests that he was in any respect an enlightened monarch.

David's last requests of Solomon (I Kings 2:1-9) are in

keeping with the life revealed in the preceding narrative. Some interpreters have thought that Solomon himself or Solomon's scribes or some later scribes wished to justify Solomon's murders by attributing them to his father's last will and testament. I am quite satisfied that Solomon needed no paternal request to do these things; but I am also quite satisfied that David may have felt some discomfort at dying with some accounts not closed because of previous services (Joab) or a promise (Shimei).

My readers may wonder why I have been so savage in smashing the plaster image of David. I trust they will notice that I have used nothing except the biblical record which began with the scribes of David and Solomon. As I remarked above, David is one of the most prominent biblical figures as well as one of the most discreditable. To deal with him as a precursor of Jesus Christ is nearly incredible; one might as well deal with Samson as a precursor of Jesus Christ. David was a precursor of Herod the Great. If one takes the trouble to read the books of Chronicles (two of the dullest books ever written), one will notice that all the features which the Chronicler found disedifying in the hero are omitted. That is the way in which many Christian interpreters have dealt with David. With a primitive theology they thought that a man who succeeded so well must have had God on his side; and if he looked at his neighbor's wife to lust after her, he wrote Psalm 51 to express his repentance. He did not write Psalm 51; and the repentance described in 2 Samuel 12:13-23 is simply a superstitious effort to avoid the death of his child. When the child dies, repentance is finished.

The danger of making David a hero is the danger of accepting the principle that success proves the approval of

God. I think the author of 2 Samual 9-20 leaned toward this principle; and he attempted, perhaps too subtly, to tell the story of great ambition and pride which issued in a ghastly failure.

CHAPTER

## 22

# WISE MAN

IN a book published a few years ago I wrote that historians think that behind the traditional wise man Solomon they can discern the historical reality of a pompous fool. In this essay I shall attempt to set forth some of the evidence which supports this belief. Readers of these chapters will probably become somewhat impatient with what appears to be a sustained effort to denigrate long venerated biblical heroes. I am aware of this, and their impatience could be avoided by remaining silent about points concerning which I have no obligation to speak. But venerating false heroes is a defect which approaches the worship of false gods.

That Solomon was a wise man seems well founded in the biblical text. When God appeared to Solomon in a dream and offered Solomon anything he would ask, Solomon asked for wisdom (I Kings 3:5-14). With wisdom God also granted Solomon riches and glory; does not any fool know that it is wisdom which obtains riches and glory? Solomon's wisdom in judgment was shown in the story of the two women and their infant sons (I Kings 3:16-28); the wise man discerns what is in the heart. The wise man makes wise sayings; Solomon uttered 3000 wise sayings and wrote 1005 songs. Most of the book of Proverbs is attributed to him, as well as the Song of Songs. It is Solomon's known wisdom and prudence which assures David that Solomon will take care of David's enemies after David is dead (I Kings 2:6,9).

Yet it is not without reason that modern interpreters, as I

243

said above, think that this traditional wisdom is the mask of a fool. We think this because the history of Solomon, scanty as it is, contains a number of references to what seems to be folly. The biblical traditions of Solomon state that the wise man became a fool in his old age, and they assign religious breakdown as a reason for this. There are good reasons for thinking that the recital of Solomon's troubles and failures in the later years of his life is artifically located. In the traditional wisdom the wise man could not fail unless he turned foolish.

The stories of Solomon contained both stories of great success and stories of great failure, and the principles of wisdom demanded that failure should follow success. The modern scholar doubts both the success and the wisdom. He explains the attribution of wisdom literature to Solomon as due to the establishment of a royal scribal office by David, continued under Solomon. Ancient kingdoms could not be administered without a large staff of scribes who prepared and preserved records in large quantities. The late Roland de Vaux argued very well that David's administration was modeled after the methods used in Egypt. The scribes were the first professional learned men, the first to write and read literature, both religious and secular; both in Egypt and in Israel the scribes prepared collections of wise sayings. Solomon was a patron of wise men, which does not make him a wise man.

Let us look at some of the achievements of Solomon of which the scribe boasts. He gives more space to Solomon's buildings than to anything else. This is not surprising; many ancient Near Eastern kings left records of their buildings, of which they were as proud as their conquests. The reader should understand that modern scholars believe that David conquered Jerusalem as his personal property, not as an annexation either to his kingdom of Judah or his kingdom of Israel. The entire city (which was not large) became the estate of the king; its people became royal slaves.

The entire city was populated by members of the "court"—officers of the royal staff, their subordinates and their slaves, the royal military bodyguard, the priests of the royal cult. Several indications suggest that most of these people were not Israelites; David and Solomon after him depended upon foreigners for the administration of the kingdoms. We mentioned in an earlier chapter the existence of conquering aristocracies in the kingdoms of the ancient Near East; we cannot surely so define the kingdoms of David and Solomon; but many of the signs of such an aristocracy appear.

Nothing of the works of Solomon remains. If we take the literary description as accurate, it appears that the temple which Solomon built was much more modest than the royal residence; but the dimensions of the royal residence are not given. It seems that the number of 700 members of his harem is exaggerated—wistfully, perhaps (I Kings 11:3); we need not think of a palace of those dimensions. It is doubtful that Solomon could have built a palace as grand as those of which we have information in Egypt, Mesopotamia and Canaan. There was no Israelite model to which it could be compared; the text tells us that Solomon had to hire foreign craftsmen, for the Israelites had never learned the skills of monumental building.

The scribe gives much more attention to the temple; for this also there was no Israelite model. The foreign workmen built a temple after a Canaanite model of which samples have been found elsewhere. The courts, unwalled and unroofed to accommodate crowds, must have been quite extensive; but the temple building proper could be placed within a modern baseball diamond—that is, a square 90 feet on a side.

Furthermore, the temple area appears to have been a part of the palace complex; just as the city itself was a royal estate, so the temple was a royal chapel. It took some time for Jerusalem to become the holy place—never as long as the kingdom of Israel endured; but the erection of the holy place was the most lasting achievement of any Israelite king. People are still quarreling about its possession. Jesus said of the third temple to stand upon Solomon's site that a stone would not be left upon a stone, as Micah and Jeremiah had said of the temple of Solomon (Micah 3:12; Jeremiah 7:13-14; 26:4-9).

According to tradition David had intended to build a temple; it is not clear why he did not. But he did intend to make Jerusalem the center of Israelite worship; this was the purpose of bringing to Jerusalem the ark of the convenant, the oldest symbol of the presence of the one God worshiped by all the tribes of the Israelite league. As we saw in a preceding chapter, David intended to subsume the convenant of Yahweh with Israel under the covenant of Yahweh with David. Few men in the Judeo-Christian tradition have known so well how to blend religion with politics. Solomon merely furnished the housing for the symbol. How successful he was appears from the unreserved readiness of the tribes of Israel to abandon the king, the ark and the temple under Solomon's successor. Whatever may have been the antiquity of the ark of the convenant—and it must have been a few hundred years—it ceased to be a symbol of the presence of God in Israel when it became the symbol of the monarchy.

Solomon was a merchant prince; there was nothing re-markable in this, for most ancient kings were merchant princes. It is quite clear of the king of Tyre, Solomon's ally and friend and partner in building enterprises and trading ventures. In the kingdom of Assyria, as in others, foreign trade was a royal monopoly; all merchants who engaged in it were licensed agents of the king. Foreign trade was a high risk and a high profit undertaking; such undertakings have never been possible except for those who have enough capital to accept the risk. Solomon's wealth is described in certainly exaggerated terms in I Kings 10:14-29. The reader will notice that most of the articles mentioned were articles of luxury trade; such articles have always been of prime concern in foreign trade. It is clear from this and from other indications that the wealth generated by Solomon's trade did not seep down into the small towns and villages where the peasants and artisans lived.

Nevertheless, from a strictly economic point of view Solomon made good use of Israel's position on the commercial lanes of the ancient Near East. The horizons of his trade extended to the Arabian peninsula, Egypt and Asia Minor, and perhaps to Africa, where some geographers think Ophir should be sought. It is somewhat strange that Mesopotamia is not included; very probably the Assyrians, great merchants as well as great warriors, had already begun to lay the foundations of the greatest trade monopoly the world had yet known.

Solomon's relations with Tyre gave him access to sources and markets accessible only by sea. His caravans traveled by the land routes on which Israel, as I have mentioned, lay. No succeeding king either of Israel or of Judah is reported to have engaged in trading with similar success; where trade was so deeply implicated with politics, the division of Solomon's kingdom into its two original components of Israel and Judah must have weakened the kingdoms commercially as well as in other ways. I trust my readers will not find tedious these references to matters of concern in the ancient Near East which are similar to matters of concern in the contemporary world. I hope I will not be thought cynical when I remark that the Israel-Arab problems were little attended to when they were questions of principle; they became matters of common concern when they became questions of trade.

There were certain political and social developments in the reign of Solomon which must be judged unwholesome. We may mention first the rise of a ruling landowning class. The existence of such a class can be seen in the books of Kings and in the books of the prophets. It does not seem unfair to attribute the rise of this class to Solomon. David and Solomon, as we have seen, depended on professional soldiers and professional administrators to manage the kingdom. These were not Israelites or Judahites, although they were not all of foreign extraction; they were "king's men," and their loyalty was rendered to their paymaster.

If the pattern which is seen in every similar political system is to be traced here, the king rewarded his officers with donations of land. Ancient Israelite custom was to retain the land in the family, and thus to prevent the acquisition of large estates. How the land came into the royal domain we do not know; the ancient scribes in this case did not know how to describe what was going on because they did not even see it; but the process has been observed often enough elsewhere to permit us to say that it is not difficult to make certain assumptions.

The small landholder, perpetually in dept to the king or the king's men, was gradually wiped out. The affairs of the towns and villages as well as local justice, once administered by the local small landholders (the elders) were now decided by the local landlord, who was one of the king's men. The ruling class may have been those for whom Solomon made gold as common as silver and silver as common as stones; they were a ruling class described with sarcasm by Amos (6:3-7) and Isaiah (5:8-14) two hundred years later. The late Roland de Vaux believed he had found the only housing of the poor ever discovered in ancient Israel at Tirzah, one of the royal cities of Jeroboam; the houses were in ruins, but at their best they must have been wretched, overcrowded slums.

Nor was it from the ruling class that Solomon extracted the taxes to support himself, his household and his "princes," as the Bible calls the "king's men." Death and taxes are not only sure things, they are also the oldest things. Ancient conquerors made things easy for their subjects and taxed their vassals for all the traffic would bear. If Solomon taxed his subjects, he did nothing new or original. I shall not attempt to sum up for my readers the scholarly discussion of Solomon's twelve districts (I Kings 4:7-19). The scribe says expressly that they were tax districts, instituted to collect the revenues to support the royal household. The support in food alone (I Kings 5:2-3) is probably not exaggerated, like the harem; the king's table fed several hundred people, if not a few thousand. This support was rendered by peasants who never saw meat except when it was alive in the hide more than a few times a year.

Ancient taxes were paid in kind, and the peasants delivered the goods to royal storehouses, generously distributed through the country. I remarked that the ancient peasant was constantly in debt up to the limit; in a bad year his yield was so close to the margin that he could lose not only his land but his wife and children, sold into slavery. It was to the same royal storehouse that the peasant would go in the next sowing season for seed grain, if he had not even produced enough surplus for seed. If he borrowed he would pay a frightful rate of interest. Between taxes and interest his entire crop must have been mortgaged before it was even in the ground. When he sat in security (I Kings 5:5), his security would endure until he was visited by the landlord, the moneylender, or the tax collector—all king's men.

A form of taxation now abandoned, but used in the ancient world and the modern world up to the nineteenth century, was forced labor. Before the invention of money, and after its invention but before its wide distribution, sovereigns imposed work upon their subjects instead of cash collections. This practice seems to have been universal throughout the ancient Near East; and it is strange that the Israelites had such a strong aversion to it. Perhaps other ancient peoples had as strong an aversion but have left no literary expression of their feelings.

Such work as the building of Solomon's palace, temple, fortifications, storehouses, stables and like projects had to be accomplished by forced labor. The scribes clearly contradict themselves, denying in I Kings 9:22 what they affirm in I Kings 5:27, that Solomon imposed forced labor on all Israelites. The demand of the tribal assembly convoked to anoint Solomon's successor that the Israelites be relieved from the burdens imposed by Solomon makes it clear that Solomon exacted forced labor; the allusion to whips leaves no doubt that it was forced labor about which they complained (I Kings 12:1-20). The account of the schism presents no motive for the rejection of the Jerusalem kingship except this; if there were other factors involved, they were not reported. I shall try in my concluding paragraphs to present a summary of a government to which rebellion was the only rational response.

As knowledge of the ancient Near East grows broader and deeper, it becomes clear that David and Solomon instituted a Canaanite monarchy. Information about these city-states shows that they were governments directed to the enrichment of a small ruling class of landowners under the patronage of a king. Even the religion of the Canaanites was a theological undergirding of an establishment of oppression. Few establishments, if any, have ever exploited a subject people as successfully as the Canaanite monarches.

The Israelite tribal league, it is thought by many, was a conscious and deliberate rejection of the institutions which supported the Canaanite system of exploitation: the monarchy, the military landowning aristocracy, and the temple. Now what they had rejected was imposed upon them by men who claimed to be the representatives of the deity. David experienced two insurrections, and the son of Solomon experienced one which deprived him of an entire kingdom. Plainly the Israelites did what they could to express disapproval. It was not enough; history was, as it so often has been, on the side of the oppressors.

There are, it seems, ample indications that the government of the "wise" Solomon was oppressive and exploitative; that it was dedicated to the enrichment of the royal household and a ruling clique; that it was cruelly indifferent to the welfare of the subjects. This is not a matter of applying modern standards of judgment to an ancient monarchy; Jeremiah could never have said of Solomon, as he said of his own contemporary Josiah, that he ate and drank and did what was right and just and dispensed justice to the weak and the poor

(Jeremiah 22:15-16). Viewed by any standards ancient or modern, Solomon, as he is described in texts written in his favor, may have been one of the worst men ever to hold political power. His own son was quoted as saying that Solomon flogged his subjects with whips. If one locates his garrison and chariot cities on the map, one observes that they were very poorly located to defend his frontiers, from which David had removed agressive neighbors; they were very well located to send flying squadrons against his subjects.

Let us turn and consider the person revealed by these same friendly scribes. It is true that ancient scribes did not concern themselves with psychology; they reported what could be seen and heard, and only from these observed details can the historian conclude what the characters thought and felt. Even with this reservation, some conclusions can be drawn from what is reported. I have said that a harem of a thousand is probably a wistful exaggeration, but we do not know how much; it is known that Ramses II of Egypt fathered 147 children, all legitimate. It does not seem unfair to say that a man who thought a harem of 700 was the height of bliss was oversexed; or if the number is exaggerated, the scribe who so much admired it was oversexed.

The dabbler in history who has visited Versailles is compelled, when he reads about Solomon, to think of Louis XIV of France; and when he thinks of Louis XIV, he is drawn to think of Louis XVI. Certainly the grand court of Versailles, where hundreds were supported in luxury and idleness, would have been to the Israelite scribe a greater example of what he called "wisdom" than the court of Solomon. Other Israelite scribes might have said that both courts invoked upon themselves a terrible judgment; the court of Versailles could have been described in the words of Amos and Isaiah which I cited above. I do not know whether Marie Antoinette ever said "Let them eat cake"; Solomon could have said it.

The scribes of this history accepted a principle of ancient wisdom which has had to be qualified. The principle, stated briefly, was that wisdom proved itself by success. It should not be necessary to argue at great length that this measures men by quite secular standards, standards which are often applied. By these standards Solomon was wise, and Jesus of Nazareth was a fool. Many have thought so, but few have dared to say it. Paul said that God has chosen the weak and the foolish of this world to confound the strong and the wise. Among the strong and the wise of this world Solomon stands out as an eminent example. Basically he was a fool.

When Jesus proclaimed an attitude toward wealth and luxury which was in direct contradiction to the "wisdom" of Solomon, he knew what he was doing. He knew that those who smash plaster idols anger those who place their trust in idols. I said above that history is usually on the side of the oppressors. It is not always; history abandoned both the dynasty of David and the court of Versailles. But the prevailing tendency of history does lend support to the view that if you want to make it in this world, you should take Solomon as your model.

# THE BEAUTY OF REVENGE

JESUS is quoted as saying, "You have heard the commandment, 'You shall love your neighbor but hate your enemy' " (Matthew 5:43). One modern version renders the Greek by "countryman" for "neighbor," perhaps restricting the meaning too narrowly. "Neighbor" means not the one who lives next door, but one who lives in the same village, the one (or rather those) with whom you have most relations in common, those who belong to your "group." I am aware of the problems of translation.

Commentators generally point out that the Old Testament contains no commandment to hate one's enemy; continuing the word study, we see that "enemy" means one who is not of your group, the stranger. If one translates one word as "countryman," the second word should be translated "foreigner." We are still not on the right track. The Hebrew and Greek words are used of personal enemies as well as of members of hostile groups. The saying of Jesus that one must love one's enemies applies both to personal enemies (who may be one's neighbors) as well as to members of hostile groups.

If there is indeed no commandment in the Old Testament saying in so many words "hate your enemies," there are certainly passages which say something other than "love your enemies." I choose as the primary example Psalm 137:8-9:

O daughter of Babylon, you destroyer, happy the man who shall repay you the evil you have done us!

Happy the man who shall seize and smash your little ones against the rock!

This is obviously addressed to members of a hostile group. But it seems to be personal enemies who appear in Psalm 69:23-29. The passage is too long to quote, but I suggest the reader find it and read it aloud. It is a formal, almost ceremonial curse delivered at length and in detail. An even longer and more detailed curse, equally ceremonial, is found in Psalm 109:6-20; the reader is invited to also read this aloud.

I select these three passages as representative of a large number of passages in the Psalms. Many of the Psalms are classified as "individual lamentations," prayers for help in various personal troubles. The help is often asked against enemies; the prayers have been broadened for general use, and it is usually impossible to specify who the enemies are or what they are doing. They are quite often, as I said above, "neighbors." The late Sigmund Mowinckel suggested that they were practicing black magic. Whoever they were or whatever they were doing, the psalms of lamentation wish them no good; the prayers are not merely that the threats be averted, but that the enemies be so damaged that they cease to be threats. When all these passages are assembled, they form a rather alarming mass of expressions of hostility. In Judaism, which regarded the Bible as a revealed way of life, the reference of Jesus to a commandment to hate one's enemy is quite faithful to the Old Testament. As I observed concerning the widom of Solomon, when Jesus contradicted certain elements in Jewish tradition he knew what he was doing.

Let us consider first the appalling imprecation of Psalm 137:8-9. We do not know how often conquering troops dashed out the brains of infants, ripped up pregnant women, and committed similar personal indignities. It seems to have been as frequent as we would expect. Such things were done by United States troops in the last war in which the United

States was engaged; they are not horrors of ancient war. The psalm is picturesque and concrete in its imagery; it is not an abstract prayer for the defeat of the enemy. Nor is it a prayer for victory for the Judahites, just for the total defeat of those who have defeated them. One may compare Mark Twain's "War Prayer." Twain, however, was writing satire; the psalmist was deadly serious. The psalm is, as I called it above, an expression of group hostility, unusual only in its viciousness.

Or is it so unusual? History and literature from their beginnings to the present contain abundant expressions of group hostility which yield but little to the imprecation upon Babylonian infants. If space permitted I would quote some of these, in spite of the fact that they would be quite offensive. I do believe space permits me to quote General Philip Sheridan's remark that the only good Indians he ever saw were dead Indians. But if we limit ourselves to the Bible, we shall find far more such expressions of group hostility than we can quote. It is remarkable that the Egyptians in the book of Exodus are not the objects of such expressions; the Pharaoh there stands for a whole people.

But if we run through the historical books of the Old Testament, we encounter enemies of the Israelites throughout: Amalekites, Maobites, Ammonites, Edomites, Philistines, Canaanites, Arameans, Assyrians, Babylonians. The diligent Bible reader will recognize the names of this enumeration. The same diligent reader will remember that they are the objects of prayer for their extermination, and of narratives recounting with glee their defeat and humiliation, if not their extermination. One may say that if mankind had never learned to hate his enemies, it would need nothing but the Old Testament to learn the lesson. Again, we see that the words of Jesus quoted above were not uttered in a void.

We cannot say that the moral revolution which the words

of Jesus initiated began immediately. In the same New Testament which begins with the Gospel of Matthew the last book is the Revelation of John. In this book the hostility of the author against the Antichrist and his followers is focused upon the historical reality of Rome. His hatred of Rome and his wishes for its destruction fall short in no respect from the classic xenophobia of so much of the Old Testament.

In choosing some passages of the Psalms for discussion, I have chosen one text (out of three) in which group hostility is involved in prayer. Students of ancient religions notice that most of the literature deals with public religion and public cult. These religions are easily identified as national or tribal. The gods belong to the group, and the group belongs to the gods. The gods have an ethnic identity; and this is the case even when the gods are associated with natural forces, which may be assumed to belong to everyone. The gods take part in war just as they take part in other group activities. There is usually one god (sometimes a goddess) who is the special patron of war, and who is invoked as the national defender; in these cults the identity of the gods with the people becomes most apparent.

In the ancient Near East this is clearest in the god Ashur, whose name appears in the city Ashur and the people Ashur (Assyria). Not only in Assyria but for other peoples religion appears as a function of politics. People pray to their own gods, aware that other peoples pray to their gods. If both groups pray to the same god, the god must make a choice. If they pray to different gods, the loser becomes a vassal of the winner. The Assyrian king Ashurbanipal thought it worth recording that he repossessed the image of Ishtar carried off to Elam 1635 years previously. As long as the Elamites had "our" Ishtar, she stood in Elam as a symbol of vassalage.

It is unfortunately true that much of the Old Testament

exhibits the same view of religion as a function of politics. This view appears in a narrative to which we have already given some attention—the story of the exodus. This, as we noticed, is the prime example of God's saving power and will. No explanation is necessary to show that this power and will is exclusively directed to the Israelites. It is not even hinted that God might have some interest in saving the Egyptians. They are charged with no crimes except oppressing the Israelites and killing Israelite male infants. The oppression, we have seen, was no more than the oppression imposed by the Egyptian monarchy upon all its subjects. Historians are sure that the genocide described in the text is completely unhistorical. The sins for which God might have been angry at the Egyptians were the invention of Israelite tradition. But the Israelite scribes would not have found it important whether the Egyptians were wrongdoers or not. They stood in the way of Israel's ambitions; that made them God's enemies.

Paradoxically, it is not the unabashed inhumanity of Psalm 137 that is theologically dangerous; the shock value of the inhumanity is so great that the reader is at once repelled by the sentiment. This is not to say that he is incapable of the sentiment, should it be his own family or his own group which is attacked. But in the calmer moods of daily life he will at once draw his mantle of self-righteousness more closely and say, "Of course that is not Christian." And it may escape him that the theological peril lies in the way in which the Psalm, the story of the exodus, and many other Old Testament texts assume without reflection that God is one of us, that he belongs to us, that he is as committed to our purposes as we are, that he would cease to be God if he did not belong to us. God is an Israelite or he is a false god.

The Old Testament is a large and complex book, and there are few themes found in it which are not submitted to some attack or criticism in other parts of it. Most of the prophets deny that God is an Israelite, or that he is committed to the desires and purposes of Israel. I believe that some writers denied even that he is committed to the survival of Israel. Among these I would include the scribe who quoted God as telling Moses that he would wipe out this people and replace it with another, not the descendants of Moses (Exodus 32:9-10). The scribe goes on to cite reasons why God ought not to do this, and thus yields to the political theology; but he did what he could, as he saw it, to maintain God's absolute freedom from human commitments. Certainly belief in God's freedom would seem to demand that God cannot be involved in our quarrels, or compelled to take sides. It seems a fairly safe general statement that in the wars and disputes of hostile groups of which we have any information there has been no side which God could take without dishonoring himself.

If this statement about taking sides between hostile groups, however large or small they may be, is true, the same statement would seem to be more easily applicable to disputes between individual persons. Probably many of my readers will find it too extreme to be accepted in either context. Surely, they will say, there must be situations in which the conflict between good and evil can be perceived in elemental terms, where one can, indeed, takes sides without compromising with evil. I wish I could find such instances; and I wish to leave no doubt that it is not mere cynicism which leads me to say this. One of the incontrovertible aphorisms of the Bible is the statement that the desires of man's heart are evil from the start (Genesis 9:21).

Let me turn, then, to the second type of interpersonal hostility which the texts exhibit, the purely personal hostility which is expressed in Psalms 69 and 109. These psalms are, as we saw above, personal lamentations; they belong to the most common type of psalm, the personal prayer for help in various troubles. Quite often the trouble is caused by personal enemies, more often than the modern devout Christian would find occasion for in his own life. I think of the prayers which used to be uttered for the victory in sports of a Catholic university, the champions of Our Lady, doing combat for the true faith against unbelievers.

In this situation imprecations like those of Psalms 69 and 109 would seem to express the sentiments of the believers quite accurately. I do not know whether the devout Christian, confronted with a personal adversary who is a threat to his promotion or to the successful completion of a sale would wish to use such prayers for his own success, prayers which are explicitly prayers for another's failure. In any case, one who utters such prayers is certainly out of harmony with the saying of Jesus that we should love our enemies and pray for our persecutors (Matthew 5:44; Luke 6:27-28). It does not seem fanciful to suppose that it is just such prayers as Psalms 69 and 109 that Jesus had in mind when he uttered this saying. What was said to the forefathers presupposes the ordinary course of human social exchange; the saying of Jesus reveals that there is a better way of life.

Is it a better way, really? Does not the saying pass too quickly over one of the greatest pleasures available to man in this vale of tears, the pleasure of glee at the fall of one's enemies? Is this not a pleasure which rivals the pleasures of love? In another psalm (54:9) the writer thanks God for affording him this pleasure. It is the other side of the pleasure which is expressed in the exultant shout of victory. If personal enmity were removed as a theme of literature, how many plays, poems and novels would be banished from our bookshelves?

Is it not in the crises of human combat that we see the supreme instances of love and compassion, of heroic self-sacrifice on behalf of others? Do we keep on reading the books and presenting the plays for the love and compassion portrayed in them, or for the pleasure of seeing vindictive violence done upon villains? The concern for violence presented on television will cease, it seems, if the violence is presented as rationally and morally justified. Revenge, if it is done upon the deserving, is indeed a way of life. Jesus has never convinced us that there is a better way.

There can be no doubt that both the prophets of the Old Testament and Jesus proclaimed God as judge and declared that he is not indifferent to the wicked things which men do to each other. Neither can there be any doubt that the sayings of Jesus clearly reserve this judgment to God and deny it to men upon each other. If we take this saying seriously, we could raise questions even about such acceptable institutions as the law, courts and the police power. I do not raise these questions here; they are too complex for treatment on the scale of ·these essays. But the saying certainly leaves no room for personal judgment of others, whether it is effective or not.

In the same order of pleasure with revenge is the pleasure of the ineffective hatred of enemies which is almost the only pleasure left to weaklings, whether the weakness comes from social position, physical inferiority or political powerlessness. When one can do nothing else but curse the offender privately, that is what one does; and one is not likely to reflect on the saying of Jesus that such apparently innocent fun merits God's verdict of condemnation.

The discussion of what appears to be a clear contradiction between the sayings of Jesus and much of the poetry and narratives of the Old Testament raises further questions which I am probably imprudent to mention here. The heretic Marcion (of the second century), as far as we know, was the first Christian to assert that there was an irreconcilable contradiction between the Old Testament and the New Testament. The God of the Old Testament was a different God from the God and father of our Lord Jesus Christ. The morality of the Old Testament was in opposition to the morality of the New Testament. Even the authentic New Testament, in Marcion's view, consisted of no more than the Gospel of Luke and a few Epistles of Paul. Marcion caused quite a stir in his day; but the church rejected him and accepted the Old Testament as the word of God.

But the church has never remained entirely firm in the position which it took against Marcion. It has long been a commonplace among Christians that the Old Testament is the rule of law, the New Testament the rule of love. Once the Old Testament is accepted as equally the word of God with the New Testament, it becomes embarrassing to speak of the abolition of the Law by Jesus—or ought to become embarrassing. Yet the words of Jesus in the Gospels compel us to say that Jesus abolished the Law; so his words are understood in the other books of the New Testament, and so the church has lived since the first century. Yet the primitive church in Palestine regarded itself as Jewish and lived in observance of the Law. Plainly not everything was always as clear as we would like to think it was.

Discussions such as those in which I have been engaged in this chapter have long been common in theology. Whatever happens to the Roman Catholic prohibition of divorce, there is no possibility that the church will return to the Old Testament law and practice of divorce at the will of the husband. Most Catholics do not know how tolerant the church has been of fornication and adultery; but it seems impossible that the church in her teaching should ever relax the uncompromising rigidity which it believes is faithful to the New

Testament. In this area the rigidity also reflects the Law of the Old Testament. In the use of violence, upon which this essay touches, the church seems to have preferred to stick to the practice of hate your enemy when he deserves it, which Jesus says belongs to the Old Law. It appears that consistency is not to be sought too avidly in the attitude of the church toward the Law.

There are two further questions which can be raised; they are not answers but rather restatements of the problems. The first question is how we are to view the unity of the Old Testament. It is surely not a single body of consistent doctrine. The prophets of the Old Testament are often in line with the teaching of Jesus and critical both of Israelite law and Israelite practice. Indeed, they are sometimes critical of the very character which God takes in Israelite belief, the character which we find portrayed in other books of the Old Testament. I have been discussing the God who became an Israelite in the exodus stories and in many of the Psalms; this Israelite God is rejected by Amos, Hosea, Isaiah and Jeremiah, not to mention others. These illustrations may help us to see that the response of Jesus to the Old Testament is not one or simple.

The second question I dealt with in an earlier chapter of this book but it has never been dealt with anywhere to complete satisfaction. The question is simply what it means to call the Bible "the word of God." It does not mean, to repeat a phrase from the preceding paragraph, that the Bible is a consistent statement of doctrine dictated by God himself. The Old Testament contains many statements of doctrine which Christians cannot believe and of morality which Christians cannot practice. It is contrived to say that God changes his character or his teaching or—as many have said—adapts both to the human condition. As far as I can tell, the bloodthirsty Israelites of David's time or the bloodthirsty Romans of Jesus' time were quite as ready for the gospel as are my contemporaries and I.

The Bible may become both more intelligible and more meaningful if it is understood less as a record of what God said than as a record of man's response to the presence and activity of God. It is in the response that God is revealed, sometimes better, sometimes not so well. We Christians think that the Old Testament cannot be understood without the New, nor the New Testament without the Old. Jews did not think so, and this is one of the basic differences between Jews and Christians. The books are written, but the presence, the activity and response endure. Man continues to learn about God and himself as long as God is present and man responds, even without knowing it.